From Underdog to Winning Bitch

My Dachshund's Lessons for Overcoming Obstacles

Virginia Weida

Aurora Corialis Publishing

Pittsburgh, PA

Cover Photo of Virginia & Heidi: Anita Buzzy Prentiss, Buzzy Photography
Cover Photo of Heidi: Jeremy Pacacha, Rolling Thunder Photography

Printed in the United States of America
Editing: Valentine Brkich, Aurora Corialis Publishing
Cover Design: Karen Captline, BetterBe Creative
Paperback ISBN: 978-1-958481-64-6
Ebook ISBN: 978-1-958481-65-3

Praise for *From Underdog to Winning Bitch*

"Virginia takes the reader on a touching and witty personal journey through pet ownership and dog training, then transforms these lessons into valuable tools for both personal and career success. Her perspective on these two distinct worlds and how they intersect makes this book unique and filled with valuable insights. Whether you are just beginning a journey, looking to make a change, or wish to recognize the value of hobbies and play, this book is for you.

"Through the years that I have had both a professional and personal relationship with Virginia and Heidi, I have seen these seven success traits from the book manifest in their lives. My favorite one, and the one I see the most from them, is motivation. Through finding success together in the ring, getting Heidi through her injury and recovery from back surgery, and the motivation to tell this story, this team is truly an inspiration to me, and I'm lucky to know them."

~ Maria Duthie
Equine & Canine Body Worker and Coach | Author of *Chocolate Cake is the Best Medicine*

"In *From Underdog to Winning Bitch*, Virginia Weida turns dog agility into a masterclass in confidence, resilience, and bold ambition. Inspired by her fearless dachshund, this book is a rallying cry for women ready to stop shrinking and start leaping—tail up, head high, and unapologetically fierce."

~ Melissa Moseley
Award-Winning Designer. Small Dog Mama. Big Believer in Bold Moves.

"Virginia Weida's book, *From Underdog to Winning Bitch*, reads like a thoughtful conversation you would have with a mentor to gain insight into honestly assessing your shortfalls to build outrageous confidence so you can enjoy your lifelong learning experience and not just its outcomes.

"Using her learning experiences in dog sports to illustrate motivation, goal setting, resilience, and winning strategies creates concrete examples in every chapter. Her success in the male-dominated commercial real estate industry is proof that her lessons work.

"And for those who like efficiency, at the end of the book, there are checklists of the points made in each chapter that will inspire and encourage you to not only compete, but win!"
~ Karen Kukish, M.B.A.
Publishing Consultant

"Virginia Weida has written a powerful book that blends the thrill of dog agility with timeless lessons in leadership, resilience, and optimism. Heidi is more than a canine star; she is a teacher of persistence and adaptability, modeling how to rise above setbacks with grace and grit. Whether you're leading a team, building a business, or navigating personal challenges, you will find strategies here to remind you that goals are attainable with preparation, vision, and unwavering belief. This book belongs in the hands of every leader who knows success is built one run, one choice, one win at a time."

~ Theresa Ream
CEO of The Ream Companies and Founder of Feminine W.I.L.E.S. Lifestyle & Business Consulting

"I've known Virginia professionally through the commercial real estate world, and reading her book gave me a whole new appreciation for her spirit and determination. I fell in love with her canine Heidi.

"Beyond the competition stories with her dog, what truly stood out were the life lessons Virginia drew from her partnership with Heidi—lessons about patience, preparation , perseverance, and believing in yourself. Her journey is inspiring and heartfelt, a reminder that success often begins with the relationships that teach us the most."

~ Terri Sokoloff, CBI, CNE, CRB, GRI
President and Broker, Specialty Group

"In starting a new career, it is often challenging to determine how to conduct yourself. Ms. Weida uses a relatable analogy to demonstrate the importance of communication, dedication, and teamwork to provide a roadmap for success in business.

"Everyone who has a pet in their life has learned something from them. Usually this is something as prosaic as, "Enjoy the simple things in life." She takes it further than that and translates what Heidi has taught her into important life and business applications.

"As someone who has experienced success in both her professional life and the dog agility arena, she is uniquely positioned to teach these lessons in an understandable and enjoyable fashion.

"This book does just that. It is a fun read that you will have a hard time putting down."

~ Lee Averbeck
Senior Web Developer, Scope Interactive

"As a dog lover, I was intrigued when Virginia talked with me about this book. How was she going to marry training her dachshunds with strategies for success in business? Would there be any natural correlation between the two worlds?

"Well, I got my answers (all very positive) and was blown away by Virginia's talent for telling a good story. Reading the book felt like I was chatting with Virginia. The comfort, security and support you feel when talking with her in person comes across on every page of this book.

"The correlations she draws doesn't feel forced or fake. Her suggested actions to achieve success were down-to-earth and straightforward. No dancing around topics with obscure psychological explanations.

"I highly recommend this book for its straightforward strategies and hardy dose of heartwarming dog stories and personal anecdotes that make the advice that much more sincere and relevant."

~ Maureen G. Ford, Director Global Real Estate, Alcoa Corp

"Virginia Weida's book has been a pleasant surprise. Easily readable, with fun, relatable stories about her cute and fluffy teammate, I can't wait to share it with friends and family members. So many motivational books can be dry and impersonal, but this one is fast-paced (like Heidi in her prime) with easy tips and tricks to apply to any journey you are on professionally. Thank you, Virginia for sharing your passion with us."

~ Samantha Ciotti Falcone, AIA, LEED AP
Owner of SCF Architecture

"Virginia Weida's *From Underdog to Winning Bitch* is a fantastic, relatable read! As a dog sport enthusiast and a goal oriented individual, I found myself audibly murmuring 'Yes! Exactly!' on more than one occasion. Weida's comparison of dog sports and career is strikingly accurate and allows the readers to really evaluate their true motivation for success. She guides her readers through personal anecdotes that illustrate how she solidified the staples for accomplishing her goals while still reiterating that success is a personal journey. As someone who tends to 'always go for the 51,' I found Weida's personal stories of partnership and goal reevaluation especially relevant. This book is a great reminder to both be prepared and enjoy the unexpected lessons along the way."

~ L. Dickson, CPDT, and The Dickson Dogs

"Virginia and Heidi's book is a powerful and entertaining adventure into the power of positive attitude and thinking. They provide important lessons and an outline for success that runs parallel for both human and canine. I am a witness to Virginia's and Heidi's agility career. I have incorporated Virginia's stunningly positive attitude and willingness to adapt to her teammate's strengths and weaknesses into our own program with winning results.

"Most notably, the positive concepts outlined in this book can easily be adapted to anyone's life as a blueprint for successes both inside and outside of the agility ring. Bravo, Virginia and Heidi!"

~ Joan M. Wilson and the WonderPoodles

"From Underdog to Winning Bitch is a must-read! Virginia recollects her dog agility journey with her first sport dog, Heidi, and details how the challenging moments along the way to earning multiple championship titles across various venues taught her valuable lessons that she has been able to apply to her successful career. Whether you understand anything about dog agility or not, Virginia is able to draw a picture and describe in detail what the reader needs to understand to apply seven pillars of competitive excellence to any situation to be successful. If there is anything you should know about Virginia, it is how much she loves dog agility and how much she values her professional success. *From Underdog to Winning Bitch* perfectly ties the two together in a way in which the reader can fall in love with the story while taking away valuable advice."

~ Meghan, MS, MBA
Dog Mom

"A heartwarming and beautifully written book about teamwork, adaptability, and how a wonderful little dog has helped overcome big obstacles, not just in the dog sport world but also in work and life. Virginia Weida will have you laughing and crying following Heidi's determination to get better and her silly antics. All the life lessons learned through Heidi's story translate into everyday obstacles in the workforce that we humans experience as well. A truly charming story on how a dog can teach you how to excel in the workforce and in everyday life."

~ Kayla Mickey, Financial Professional and Dog Mom

"As someone new to the agility competition world and a career woman myself, the theme of 'Underdog to Winning Bitch' piqued my interest. I found the book to be well-written and easy to follow. I flew through the pages, relating to the words and feelings the author put down about the motivation, mentality, and teamwork needed to achieve success in the world of dog sports and in the workplace. I appreciated seeing the steps needed to create a goal outline and how that was used to follow through to reach the goal which had been set.

"Sometimes we go through daily motions not realizing we've become ingrained in the process of reaching a goal without noticing we're stuck or tiring of a particular step, hindering our progress forward. In this book, Virginia explains that breaking it down into smaller goals and writing these steps down can help keep you on track and give you accountability, which can be seen, not just pushed to the back of the mind for a later date. I think anyone who feels fatigued with getting to the finish line might benefit from reading this book."

~ Chrissy B.
Real Estate Professional and Dog Mom

"If you're a dog person, this book is for you. If you're into dog sports, it will truly resonate. But anyone who could use a nudge toward becoming the best version of themselves will benefit from the story of Virginia and Heidi, her spirited agility dachshund whose career was cut short by a spinal injury.

"Their journey, filled with lessons on setting actionable goals and cultivating resilience through positivity, is a master class in winning strategy. I've known Virginia for years through the intersection of our dog agility and professional worlds, and she has a rare ability to run any course, in the ring or in her successful commercial real estate career, with grace, grit and an upbeat attitude.

"This book will help you define and chart your own course to success – and give you the confidence to adapt when life doesn't go according to plan."

~ Angie Carducci, Communications Professional and Italian Greyhound Rescue Volunteer

"A Clever, Inspiring Blend of Grit, Training, and Triumph

"This book is such a refreshing read! The author brilliantly parallels her experience training and competing with her determined Dachshund to the challenges of building credibility and success as a woman in a male-dominated business world. Her stories are honest, funny, and deeply insightful — showing how patience, consistency, and resilience apply equally to handling a headstrong pup and breaking professional barriers.

"It's not just about dogs or business — it's about mindset. The lessons translate seamlessly from the training ring to the boardroom, reminding readers that success often comes down to preparation, persistence, and a little bit of attitude (or a lot if you're a Dachshund). A must-read for anyone who appreciates strong storytelling and real-world wisdom, especially women striving to lead with confidence and authenticity."

~ Shiloh Shaver
Vice President of Business Development, CSHQA

Table of Contents

Introduction

It was just a typical Monday in April 2023. I came home from a dog training class with my youngest pup to the usual clamor for attention from my other three dogs. Except I only saw two. Where in the world was Heidi? As the dominant dog in our four-dog household, she was always first in line for food, treats, and love. Peeking outside to our sunporch off of our kitchen (everyone's favorite room in the house), I saw Heidi just sitting in the middle of the floor. I called her, but she didn't budge. Oh no! As I got closer, I noticed her eyes were wide, the size of dinner plates, and she wasn't up wiggling her butt and wagging her tail. I suspected right away what was wrong—a spinal disc injury, which dachshunds and other long-backed dogs can be prone to. My heart pounding, I scooped her up and took her out to the backyard to see if she had any movement in the grass. Nothing. She just sat there. So, I gently got her back into my arms, grabbed a towel to swaddle her for the ride, and immediately left for the emergency vet office. Time is of the essence with suspected disc and spinal cord injuries.

After a multi-hour wait (which is typical at the pet ER), while barely holding it together, we finally got to see the intake crew. My worst fears were realized—Heidi was indeed paralyzed in her back legs. They kept her overnight for observation, and she would see a neurologist in the morning for further examination. That drive home without her was awful. Would she need surgery? Would she ever walk again? Would she even survive? A few days earlier, she was running some of her fastest times in agility and having the time of her life. Just like that, her career, and possibly even her life, was over.

The neurologist confirmed that Heidi had a disc injury, and with surgery, she could gain up to ninety percent of her mobility back. After undergoing an MRI to confirm the diagnosis, they immediately took her into surgery to remove not one, but two blown discs in her lower spine. She would come home with a bag full of medications and require strict crate rest for eight weeks.

How could I possibly carry on in my work and life while this weighed on my mind? I began opening up to my clients and friends, and sharing social media posts about her situation. The outpouring of support in return was incredible! As Heidi recovered, I realized that I needed to stop building walls between my hobbies and my work. The clarity of realizing how disconnected I had become, ignoring all the gifts that Heidi had taught me, was the seed of this project. While she was recovering physically, I began laying the groundwork for sharing our story with others.

During the pandemic, when things got quiet, along with some significant health challenges that Heidi faced, I came to realize the incredible impact she and canine sports have had on my professional career: understanding and learning resilience, adaptability, leadership, teamwork, advocacy, overcoming the fear of failure... the list goes on and on. Because of my relationship and experiences with her, I have had greater career success than I ever thought possible!

After years of working in a male-dominated industry, I am driven to support women and help them become the best version of themselves, and I can't wait to share the lessons I have learned for success.

Do you feel like you are constantly being underestimated? Are you considering making a change in your life, and need a boost of confidence? Are you yearning for greater recognition? Are you starting a new venture and feeling a little lost? Are you ready to learn how to transform from underdog to winning bitch?

Then this book is for you. And of course, if you love animals, specifically dogs, then this book is definitely for you!

This book will not teach anyone how to do dog agility (I am by no means an expert!), but you will definitely learn about the sport along the way. It uses dog stories and personal experiences as examples to demonstrate and inspire readers to seek greater success in their work and life. A quick note about the title: a "winning bitch" does not need to be a spiteful, overbearing woman, as society has defined this phrase. Nor am I referring to the use of the term to imply someone as a submissive follower. Remember, in the dog world, bitch simply means the female of the dog species.

Competing with Heidi taught me that being a winning bitch means confidently overcoming challenges, communicating effectively, and building meaningful connections, primarily through greater authenticity. As you read this book, I hope you become more "am-bitch-ous" and develop the desire to be a winning bitch!

This book is part memoir and completely motivational. Through storytelling and analogy, I try to help you understand and develop confidence, become empowered, and seek greater opportunity and recognition through the unlikeliest of teachers: Heidi, the fourteen-pound, long-haired miniature dachshund.

Photo Credit: Virginia Weida

I admit that I have probably become a "crazy dog lady" over the last few years.

The truth is, I have always loved dogs, and as I've gotten older, they have become a significant part of my life. It wasn't always this way. My household growing up had a Siamese cat that ruled the house, and she lived to be over twenty years old. She came to live with us because she didn't get along with a dog in her previous household, which meant I could never have one while she was around.

My first job was as a newspaper carrier for the neighborhood, taking over the local route as my brothers outgrew it. I loved the flexibility of being able to plan my route to end at the houses that had my favorite dogs. I would often stay and play with them after I finished my deliveries. So, even though I didn't have a dog in the house growing up, I was still able to get my dog fix through neighborhood dogs, friends' dogs, occasional pet sitting, and even summer camps. Anywhere I went, I would find the dog!

It was not until I graduated from college that I got my first dog as a gift from my future mother-in-law. After graduation, we visited a shelter and came home with a puppy I named Roxanne (after the Police song, of course). Roxanne was way more dog than I could handle as a new dog owner. She was strong-willed, independent, and had a tendency to chew on anything, whether it was her toys or a precious keepsake. She was extraordinarily athletic and suffered from separation anxiety when left alone. So, my new husband and I decided she could use a canine companion to keep her company. When Roxanne was two years old, we adopted our second dog from the same shelter. Enter Iggy (named after Iggy Pop), who came home at six weeks old and was smaller than a shoe! Both Roxanne and Iggy lived long lives and were there as our two daughters were born and raised.

Roxanne passed at sixteen and a half, and Iggy lived to be seventeen and a half. The last summer that Iggy was alive, the girls and I convinced my husband that it was time to consider getting another dog. We had some friends with a few dachshunds, and we were in love with the breed. Within a few days of gaining my husband's buy-in for a new puppy, our neighbor's daughter mentioned a family that had a small litter of dachshunds they were looking to rehome.

So, within a week, we came home with Heidi. At fifteen weeks old, Heidi was the quintessential dachshund puppy. She was precocious, independent, stubborn, extraordinarily energetic, playful, and constantly testing our limits. I signed up for a puppy training class and realized that Heidi was a quick learner and extraordinarily fast.

When we started training in agility, I was simply looking for an outlet for Heidi's excessive energy and a way for us to develop a stronger bond. I had no idea about what was to come. As we progressed through our entry-level classes and training, it became clear that Heidi would be a formidable competitor if I could only learn to work with her independent streak and harness her grit and determination for good. I felt up to the task. I believed I could match her grit, determination, and stubbornness, and not give up on our team when the going got tough. We became relentless together. When Heidi was younger, she loved nothing more than going out early on the weekend and playing with me, no matter the activity.

Over the years, our journey competing in canine sports definitely had its share of ups and downs. From 2013 to 2023, Heidi and I competed together in many canine sport venues until her agility career came to an abrupt halt due to emergency back surgery. Little did I know from our modest beginnings that we would wind up competing once a month, driving over an hour each way to local competitions.

As my family dynamic changed and my kids grew and moved on to college, I had more time to try different sports with Heidi. During her career, she earned three Agility Championship Titles (almost four), and over a hundred titles overall in a variety of venues, including Teacup Dog Agility Association (TDAA), Tricks, Canine Performance Events (CPE) Agility, CPE Speedway, CPE Scent, Canine-Work and Games (CWAGS) Scent, Universal Canine, Barn Hunt, and Rodeo Dog. She's the definition of a winning bitch and has more letters after her name than a tech bro! I also developed an excellent network of "dog friends" and really enjoyed all the different events we attended.

Since bringing Heidi home in 2011, we've also adopted Penny, then Le Beau, and Gus Gus, all long-haired miniature dachshunds. We had a fabulous four-pack for a few years! Penny and Le Beau both passed away in 2024 as senior dogs (both almost sixteen years old), and I enjoyed doing scent work with both of them as they aged. Gus Gus is now my current agility partner, and Heidi is mostly retired from canine sports. Though I love them all dearly, Heidi was my original dog to learn canine sports with and the primary focus of the stories in this book.

As I came to terms with Heidi's health challenges during her recovery, I reflected on all the gifts that participating in canine sports has given me in my entrepreneurial life as a woman business owner, and the seeds of this book were planted. In the following pages, you'll get to meet Heidi and discover seven traits for success. I'll also share some stories that will detail the transformation from underdog to winning bitch, as well as Heidi's antics, and celebrate her triumph over medical setbacks. I hope that you'll be inspired by the power of authenticity and seek out moments outside your routine that remind you of the power of play, perseverance, and connection.

(L to R) The Fab Four: Gus Gus, Le Beau, Penny, Heidi
Photo Credit: Virginia Weida

Chapter One - Motivation

My first obedience class with Heidi was amazing! She was brilliant and adorably cute, and she mimicked the instructor's dog perfectly, hoping to receive as many treats as possible. When socialization time started, she ran fast circles around the classroom. "Wow! She's really fast for such a small pup," I heard again and again. "You should check out agility. I bet she'd be great!" Turns out they offered those classes at the same dog training club. So, as soon as Heidi turned a year old, we signed up for our first agility class.

She was a quick learner and fearless, so we breezed through the intro classes, and I fell in love with the sport. After we had been training together for about a year, I thought Heidi and I were ready to start competing. We were doing well enough in class, and the first trial we entered was at our home training club, which felt safe and comfortable. As it turned out, however, our first agility trial experience was incredibly humbling. Many others may have given up right then and there. Yet, I was not ready to give up—the thought didn't even cross my mind!

I knew that we had the skills and abilities to be successful, despite our disastrous debut. I may have been even more motivated by failure than by success, because it had now become a challenge to overcome. I had to persevere more than my thirteen-pound dachshund. Thankfully, we were not in competition with each other; we needed to learn to work as a team. Headstrong, persistent, tenacious, and clever—these are some of the personality characteristics that Heidi and I share. I had met my match head-on and was motivated to find a way to win—together.

Motivation is entirely personal and utterly unique from person to person. This is my story of the inspiration that helped shape my unwavering perseverance. I hope it inspires you to understand yours!

I have had dogs my entire adult life, ever since graduating from college. When I left my last job and started my home business in 2006, I was careful to make sure the dogs did not bark much during work calls. I also made sure my daughters knew not to interrupt me when my office door was closed. I was concerned that it would not be acceptable to many of my corporate clients. They were expecting professional service and didn't necessarily want to talk on the phone to a working mom with babies and dogs in the background.

However, during the COVID-19 pandemic, everyone's comfort level with working from home changed. Suddenly, everybody was surrounded by children, animals, and other family members, and the authenticity of our communication became so much more real. No longer were we shushing our kids or shooing our pets. Sometimes they even became the stars of the conversation because we were all aching for connection.

With my children grown, my dogs became the main characters in my life. It opened the door for me to be more authentic, and my different "selves" began to align. As a sole proprietor, my name is my brand, and my social media is carefully crafted with that in mind. When I posted about work, people were supportive. But when I shared posts about my dogs, people went nuts! Since some of the barriers had come down around working from home, I now felt much more comfortable sharing things outside of my work projects, and it felt great. People were taking notice and constantly asking about my dogs, which I love to talk about!

During this same period, many dog events (just like professional events) were cancelled or postponed, and Heidi's health began to decline. I was unsure whether the change in our routine was affecting her or if it was something else. She began sleeping more and needed to be carried up the steps for meals. Heidi was turning ten at the time, and I thought she was just naturally aging out of sports. On top of that, we weren't active much beyond some short outside walks.

However, I soon noticed that the hair on her belly and tail was thinning, and she began drinking a lot of water. So, off to the vet we went. After several rounds of testing, Heidi was eventually diagnosed with Cushing's Disease. Her adrenal glands were producing too much cortisol, causing her extreme lethargy, thirst, and hair loss. This condition is not curable, and it can shorten their lifespan, but it is treatable. We began daily medication, and within just a few weeks, her energy had returned. Thankfully, Heidi seemed to be back to normal (i.e., driving us all a little crazy with her energy).

As more events were being scheduled and Heidi's energy returned, we began training and competing again. I had almost given up on earning a championship title with her in CPE due to the pandemic and her declining health. But Heidi had other plans. After a ten-month pause, she returned to agility stronger than ever, and soon earned her first championship in CPE agility in November 2021, running some of the fastest times of her career! Heidi's medications had given her a second wind. We competed through all of 2022 and into April of 2023, with fast times and lots of hugs and kisses. I wondered how long she had been feeling off due to Cushing's Disease, and I was grateful we found a treatment that made her feel like herself again.

But then our career together in agility came to an abrupt and unexpected end. We were within seven qualifying runs (out of forty total required) of earning Heidi's second championship in CPE when emergency back surgery ended her career. It was during Heidi's long recovery from surgery that I had time for self-reflection. While she recovered physically, I had to recover mentally from the sudden end to our agility journey. I loved competing with her, and I was mourning the loss of our favorite sport and activity. I was also missing the time I spent with my friends in the agility community. That said, I'm an optimist, and once I realized Heidi was going to recover, I couldn't stay down for long. I began to realize how much I had grown during our journey, and I was so proud of the amazing things we had accomplished together. It motivated me to keep pushing forward, despite the situation.

I have been successful in my industry for many years, but it was my hobby with Heidi that taught me the most about how to be a winning bitch.

Competing in agility with Heidi changed my life in profound ways. My former career and volunteer experiences had given me the initial strength and faith to take a chance and try the sport. Leaning into agility with Heidi helped forge many other key traits that are essential to success, including goal setting, resilience, and adaptability, among others. I became more confident overall and began sharing more of my authentic self with everyone.

Pets live authentically and are unapologetically true to themselves. Over the many years as Heidi's partner, I realized that a winning bitch personality doesn't have to be loud. People will take notice because you're confident and have an unflappable attitude in the face of adversity. Being a winning bitch doesn't have to be flashy; instead, it has a strong spirit of resiliency and strength. This comes from the key pillars of persistence, perseverance, and passion. These pillars are interrelated and work together to help us stay motivated, smash our goals, and achieve success, contributing to a more confident and fulfilling life.

Persistence

Persistence is something that dogs naturally excel at, and Heidi is at the top of her game. Dogs stare you down when you are eating food they want. They continually remind you when they feel that they are due a cookie or reward. They decide when you wake up in the morning to let them out and feed them breakfast. They demand that you play ball or engage in an activity with them, even if you've just finished playing or if you try to ignore them because it's not a good time for you. Their persistence is truly remarkable, and we can learn a great deal from them.

My first dog, Roxanne, was the most persistent creature I had ever met, and because of that trait, she often ended up getting her way. Toward the end of her life, she was no longer able to get up on our bed, so she slept on the floor beside us. She was just under forty pounds, so when she was ready to get up and start the day, she would not take no for an answer. She would begin by scratching on the bedroom door. Then she would scratch on the bedframe itself. Then she would nuzzle her nose under the covers on my side of the bed. Then she would put her paws up on my side of the bed to try to wake me up. When all of that failed, she would literally ram the bed with her body until I got up. We had two young children at the time, and our sleep was precious, so I was always hoping for a few more minutes of rest. But no matter how much I pretended to be asleep and tried to ignore her, Roxanne always seemed to come out on top. Heidi is also incredibly persistent, but honestly, all of my dogs have been, especially when it's close to mealtime!

There were times when Heidi's persistence was helpful, as she was always up for going on an adventure to a new place. Yet her persistence could also be challenging when she found a new smell that she could not leave, or when she wouldn't respond to my handling cue and chose her own agility courses instead. I'll never forget the time we encountered a tough obstacle discrimination challenge on a course: a tunnel opening right next to the dogwalk contact. We sometimes jokingly referred to these as "traps." Some traps are too enticing, and dogs may choose which one they prefer in the moment and ignore your handling cue. But the course is designed by the judge for the dog to take one or the other; it's not the dog's choice.

On that day, Heidi refused to go through the tunnel and continued up the dogwalk, finishing on the other side of the room. I got her back with me and tried the tunnel again, sending her two more times while I varied my handling leading up to the "trap." Each time, she persistently chose the dogwalk. The fourth time, I finally got her to enter the tunnel. Hooray! Except she didn't come out the other end. And she didn't pop out at the start either. So I got down on the floor at the end of the tunnel and looked in.

To my surprise, there was a puddle of dog pee from a dog before her, and Heidi was sitting inside the tunnel on the other side. Her look told me everything: "This was why I didn't want to come in here in the first place! Now what do you want me to do?" I had to coax her out of the tunnel entry and then helped clean up the mess. I never thought to consider that there was a reason why she was not going in the tunnel, other than openly choosing to ignore my direction. We were both persistent in getting what we wanted, and in the end, it didn't work for either of us. It was a stalemate! It works much better when we are on the same side and overcoming obstacles together.

I'm sure my family has many stories about my persistence as a child. If I were told "no," for example, I would look for ways to turn that "no" into a "yes." As it turns out, two of the biggest motivators for me are hearing "no" and being underestimated. These rarely make me turn back or change direction; instead, they are signs that I am on the right track!

Persistence is the ability to keep trying when facing obstacles or setbacks.

Just as I didn't give up after our disappointing agility debut, I didn't give up when we faced challenges along the way. They made me dig in and work harder. This same behavior has helped me beyond agility. When the going gets tough, I don't surrender. I work harder and smarter to effect change, recognizing that it's always better to have the team moving in the same direction. When items for a project have a delayed delivery timeline, I look for alternative solutions and workarounds. When permit drawings are delayed in approval and the project's construction schedule exceeds the finish date, I work with the client to find a solution for remote working, ensuring their business continues to operate. When a client is hesitant about starting a project, I stay in touch and answer their questions to hopefully turn their "no" into a "yes." Optimism fuels my persistence, and I believe that my efforts will pay off, just as they did with Heidi in agility. Where some may find obstacles discouraging, I find them motivating. When you hear "no," it could just be "not yet."

Perseverance

Persistence is a day-to-day determination that builds a strong foundation for perseverance, which is a broader, overarching concept that spans a longer time frame. Perseverance is not just about rejecting "no" for an answer, but more about moving forward anyway, day by day, despite the situation or advice that you've been given. Though coaches and mentors are essential and their feedback is vital to consider, you also need to develop confidence to make the choices that are best for your journey.

Persistence in agility training is showing up to class for every session. Professionally, it's doing your work on time and following through on your commitments. Perseverance involves having a strong belief in yourself and taking steps to achieve your goal. It's about moving forward, rebounding from setbacks, and reaching your goals, despite unfavorable odds and delayed wins.

Heidi and I both had persistence, but I still wondered if we could persevere through a challenging time. We qualified and participated in our first (and only) national agility competition in 2018. It was for the Teacup Agility Association (TDAA), which was the only venue we were competing in at the time. Held in nearby Ohio that year, the competition consisted of ten runs total held over three days. That year, to earn an invitation, you had to earn a qualifying run, or "Q," in a specific standard run at a trial, which was a more challenging course than usual. We actually qualified multiple times, with the last Q actually earned at the site of the TDAA competition. Before the event, I was imagining that we would get a handful of qualifying runs and was looking forward to spending time with my dog friends and cheering them on to victory. I knew the competition would be tough, so I was keeping my expectations in check. I felt prepared.

We arrived on the morning of the trial, got all set up, and were ready to play. But day one did not go as planned. One game relied on weave pole performance repeatedly in a single run, and Heidi would complete the weave poles just once per run for me (a fairly standard expectation). In another game, she made the opening jump and then spent the time sniffing the perimeter until the clock ran out. The dogs were all new to us, and we had only visited this location once before. I'm also sure I was nervous. Looking back on it now, she behaved exactly as expected, considering all the factors.

The next day, we experienced more of the same. Two straight days with no qualifying runs! In our five years of competing together, that had never happened to us before. The daily drive back and forth to Ohio was long, and I began to question my sanity. Why should we go back if we can't win? It was a frustrating time, and I began to lose confidence. But despite all of our previous runs, I still had a glimmer of hope.

Despite those challenging and discouraging first two days, we came back for the third day of the competition, and I felt hopeful. Many of the initial barriers to our success had been overcome. The venue was no longer new to us; Heidi knew all of the dogs by that point, and the smells had all been smelled. When it was our turn, we laid down a blistering (for us) clean run for our first event of the morning! It felt great, and we both had confidence in our performance.

So, imagine my surprise when we did not qualify, having exceeded the standard course time by just a few seconds. Although we did not earn a ribbon, I still consider that run to be a wildly successful effort. We persevered despite the situation, each of us doing our best and overcoming the setbacks. We also did not let the lack of success in that event determine our future path, and we went on to have many more qualifying runs over the next five years.

Perseverance can be bold and active, but it can also be quiet strength.

In addition to her natural persistence, Heidi demonstrated remarkable perseverance following her back surgery. She accepted assistance and allowed us to carry her from crate to crate to keep her safe. She persevered in trying to move on her own shortly after her surgery. Remaining paralyzed was never an option for her. She endured treatments and medicines to help her heal. She persevered not only to walk again, but also to continue participating in activities outside her home. Although she still requires assistance with stairs, she is now otherwise fully mobile, with high energy and the occasional zoomies, despite her past challenges. If you didn't know her history, it would not be obvious.

Although Heidi's agility career ended in April 2023, she has since gone on to earn titles in other activities. She still thoroughly enjoys doing a few laps in the agility ring (without any equipment), just like the old days. She persevered to recover strongly, and we worked together through her injury by continuing to engage her in opportunities that she could participate in. She is also beating the odds with her Cushing's diagnosis. While most dogs succumb to the disease within two years after diagnosis, Heidi is now in year four! We know we are on borrowed time, but we still try to make the best of it.

In my professional life, perseverance means pushing through a deadline when your equipment has failed and you have to scramble to overcome the challenge. Perseverance is the belief that you will have success in pursuing a new job, certification, or even an industry award. On three separate occasions, I applied for industry awards but was unsuccessful in winning. In each case, I waited a year or two to gain more experience, seek feedback from my mentors and peers, and reapply. And in all three cases, I was successful the second time around. I found Heidi's perseverance in the face of adversity incredibly motivating, and realized that I rely on the same thought patterns to keep moving forward.

It's essential to clarify that perseverance and the drive to succeed require hard work and discipline. That said, it does not mean you need to work 24/7, 365 days a year. Perseverance can often be more mental than physical, and it helps maintain motivation to reach your goals. Don't confuse working long hours with having a strong work ethic. They don't necessarily mean the same thing! In this journey of life, consider doing things in moderation. Sure, I enjoy competing in canine sports with Heidi, but I balance that with running a successful company and participating in family activities. It doesn't mean I'm all in on any one thing to the exclusion of others.

Passion

Passion is a wonderful emotional construct that is challenging to define. Passion is what drives you. It's what makes you excited to get out of bed in the morning. It's an internal feeling that can't be ignored. Passion can also bring you fulfillment. You can be passionate about one thing or many, and it's not just restricted to one part of your life. When combined, passion and optimism serve as the invisible fuel that keeps us going and supports our persistent efforts to keep moving forward every day. Perseverance takes that daily persistence to the next level, with a sustained commitment to success, even in the face of adversity. All of these elements combine to create motivation, and once you gain momentum, it builds and cycles itself. Once you notice it, you will become aware that it impacts many facets of your life.

For as long as I can remember, I have been volunteering for causes that I am passionate about. As a business owner, I make time to create a social impact through volunteering with national organizations, advocating for the interior design profession, supporting local communities and small businesses, and uplifting women. These are some of the things I am passionate about through my work. You already know that I am passionate about dogs in general and dog sports as an activity, but I also enjoy music, traveling, crafts, photography, and wine tasting. I'm passionate about my family, my career, and my hobbies, and I'm currently in my dog sports era. I honestly don't know what else, besides passion, would motivate us to get up before dawn and drive more than an hour to participate in a game with our dogs. Emotional involvement and commitment are hallmarks of success.

Naturally, you may be thinking that competing with a dog means the two of us against the world. That could not be further from the truth! Second to the deep relationship and memories you create with your dog, it's the relationships with the people in the community in dog sports that make you want to keep coming back. If you love dogs, competing in dog sports lets you hang out with other dogs all the time! What could be better than that? But beyond the dogs, you get to meet handlers from all over. Dog handlers are a fascinating group of people because they share a common passion for dogs and dog sports. Beyond that, they can be incredibly different from each other.

Outsiders may also think that we compete in agility to earn ribbons, especially when they look at our pictures. It's easy to see success when you bring home some ribbons, and they are always lovely to get, as opposed to going home empty-handed. But as a competitor, the ribbons are not the real motivation at all. The wins do not determine your worth. Agility is not about the ribbons; it's about enjoying the journey with your best friend. There is a banner that hangs in our training center that reads, "Here is one last great truth … the time will come much too quickly when you will gladly give back every Q, every placement, and every title, just to be able to take your dog to the start line one more time. Enjoy the ride. Appreciate your partner. It's just a game."

Photo Credit: Virginia Weida

Winning Motivation Strategies:
- **Embrace your authentic self.**
- **Lean into your passions.**
- **Persevere through adversity.**
- **Seek community and connection.**

HEIDI'S PAWS FOR THOUGHT:

Follow your heart's desires.

Chapter Two - Goals

Heidi and I didn't start out as a winning team. At the outset, our goal seemed simple enough to achieve: enter an event, run around the ring doing a few things in order, and win a pretty ribbon! The reality was that when we entered our first event, we completely flopped. When it was our turn, my heart was pounding as Heidi and I stepped to the start jump together. I was hoping that we could complete the beginner course easily. Heidi, however, had other plans, and she decided it was the perfect time to have a case of the zoomies! She loved the small audience's attention as she ran fast circles around the room, ignoring me and all of the agility equipment. When our time was up, I even had trouble collecting her to leave the ring for the next team. I was utterly embarrassed by our performance, but my partner was exuberant. She'd had a blast!

I had grossly underestimated our readiness, the amount of work required to reach our goal, and the difficulty of the sport, while simultaneously overestimating our natural abilities. Heidi and I did not share the same goals yet. We were in it for ourselves, and we weren't working as a team. But neither of us is one to back down from a challenge, and it was clear that more work was needed from both of us to achieve our goal of winning.

Goals establish your path to success and are a key to winning. Setting and achieving your first goals can seem straightforward initially, especially when starting any venture, agility or otherwise. In agility, you sign your dog up for training classes, learn to do some skills (both human and canine), put in some practice, and start to compete. Once you become more involved, however, you realize that the skills are more complex than you thought (for both humans and canines), the competitions may be more challenging than you expected, and it's easy to feel overwhelmed quickly. The more you learn, the less you know!

Let's compare this experience with a goal most of us have shared: getting your first job. You sign up for a specific training program or attend college, learn all the necessary skills, and then apply for an open position. Easy, peasy! But once you start researching companies, you realize that there are limited (or too many) opportunities, the qualifications required may still be beyond your skillset, reaching a decision-maker is complicated, and the competition is fierce. It's easy to feel overwhelmed quickly (and we aren't even talking about what happens when you start that new job).

Amazingly, becoming overwhelmed is not something that seems to happen to Heidi. She is headstrong and confident when trying something new, and she's enthusiastic about continuing to move forward. In other words, she's a great role model!

In dog agility, competitors select the events they would like to participate in with their canine partner. Depending on the venue, there are opportunities for local, regional, national, and sometimes even international competitions for the top teams. When I thought Heidi and I were ready, I signed us up for our first local agility competition. After all, I believed I had done everything right to prepare: I had paid for the training classes and learned about the venue, and we had practiced weekly for about a year. So, I naively believed we were ready to enter our first competition. I believed my goal of earning a qualifying score for our run was readily attainable.

It turned out that my team was not aligned on the goal (i.e., Heidi had her own ideas!), and we struggled a bit at our agility debut. The goals I set were initially much more challenging to reach than I had anticipated. We did, however, earn one qualifying run out of three runs total, which was enough to keep me coming back for more. Looking back, I can safely say that although our agility career was not without its struggles at times, Heidi's overall attitude and approach motivated me to work harder to set more realistic goals for our team (both easy and stretch goals) while simultaneously pushing back against the fear of failure.

Even in the early days, I realized that I could learn a lot from my tiny but mighty teammate.

Goals in sports are not that different from goals in business. Athletes strive to achieve a personal best or win a competition, just as business leaders create plans to outperform their competitors in sales or market reach. A winning vision is fundamental to setting those goals. To the casual observer, the goals in dog agility may appear obvious at first: pay the entry, run the event, and win! It's just as easy to do this in business, too, right? Choose your next project, do the work, and win! Or what about in life? Set the goal, follow the rules, and magically achieve that goal!

I hope you realize I'm being sarcastic. There are entire books and courses about the process of goal setting for success. This chapter is not intended to cover the breadth of that knowledge but rather to share my experience and awareness of how working with Heidi and setting goals in agility have significantly impacted and improved my life. My aim is to encourage you to consider goal-setting in new and creative ways. Together, let's explore the synergies of goal setting in dog sports, business, and life.

SMART Goals

Write those goals down! Setting goals helps us track progress. Goals are not static; they should be evolving, changing, and expanding. It is hard to achieve any goal—small or large—unless you mark or acknowledge the goal and your work toward it. Otherwise, you may waste valuable time and energy with no direction. Convention also informs us that the best goals are SMART: Specific, Measurable, Achievable, Relevant, and Time-Based. When it comes to achieving your goals, each of these qualities is vital for success and deserves your consideration.

Here is the basic outline for how to set and plan for reaching your goals:

Goal: _____
    Actionable Step 1: _____
    Actionable Step 2: _____
    Actionable Step 3: _____

First, establish the goal. Next, list two or three actions or steps that you can take to work toward that goal. The hardest step is often the first! Our most significant goals require actionable steps that help us break them down into smaller, manageable parts. If your goal is to run a marathon, for example, you don't just sign up for one, buy some shoes, and run 26.2 miles. Instead, there are many steps that enable us to build, evolve, and expand to achieve these types of significant goals.

So, how do you begin? The following are some helpful questions I ask as I set goals for work or just life in general:

- Is the goal specific?
- Can it be measured? Tracking progress is important.
- Is this goal achievable? Remember, stretch goals are essential, but impossible goals can be demotivating.

- Is this goal relevant to my overall work/life direction and purpose? While a goal can push us to try new things and begin new career directions, it's important to make sure the goal won't cause our other responsibilities to go off track.
- Are there any known obstacles to overcome?
- Is there a set completion date? It can take us longer to get something done if we don't set a date.

Recognize that not all goals are immediately obtainable. We need to set goals for different purposes with a range of completion timelines that support our success. Short-term goals are quicker to achieve than longer (or lifetime) goals. For example, a common goal in my industry is to become a principal or a shareholder of a company. That would be a multi-year or even a lifetime goal, as opposed to a shorter-term goal, such as finding a new job, getting promoted, or earning a new certification.

If you are more right-brained (i.e., creative) like me, it can become arduous to sit down, put pen to paper (or even virtually with our devices), and list our goals and the steps to achieve them. But I do find joy in checking that box when the goal is achieved! For me, working toward a deadline has always been extremely motivating. Therefore, establishing a clear timeline is central to my success.

I encourage you to try these steps for a goal you're having difficulty starting; even taking one step is moving in the right direction. As daunting as it may be to list goals, action steps, and deadlines (depending on your personality), doing so is critical in helping you achieve that winning vision and mental attitude. When you list your goals, you become more intentional and more explicit about what you want. Doing so also helps you stay on track to juggle all the responsibilities in life, including your family, work, and hobbies. Participating in the sport of agility has taught me to set and track my progress toward various goals. As a result, Heidi and I achieved a great deal together (over one hundred titles!).

Let me share some more about how goals work in agility. Once your team has trained well enough to compete, you learn that every venue has a set number of achievements (i.e., qualifying runs, or "Qs") required to earn a title. When you first start on this journey, you may believe that earning titles is your primary goal. All venues offer Beginner or Novice levels, Intermediate or Open levels, Superior or Excellent/Master levels, and beyond. Some venues are designed to accommodate any dog. In contrast, others are geared toward small or "teacup" dogs, utilizing smaller-scale equipment and shorter courses (which we have competed in); still others are designed for larger dogs with longer courses. It is up to you, the handler, to study each venue and determine which ones best match your team's abilities.

Each venue you participate in offers a tracking chart showing how many Qs you need to earn titles. These charts support goal setting and tracking. It's literally a roadmap to success! You can enter each event knowing how many qualifying runs you need to reach your next goal, with the top goal on the tracking chart being the championship title. Here is a simplified version of what a standard title sheet might look like for the first level:

Beginner/Novice Level (Three Qualifying Scores required)

Date/Judge/Time or Score/Placement

    1.

    2.

    3.

Notice how much it looks like our commonly accepted SMART goal-planning steps? My years competing in agility with Heidi across three venues heartily reinforced the process of setting goals and the satisfaction that comes with completing them. Though the tracking was cumbersome at times, it was tremendously satisfying to enter qualifying runs to check the boxes for earning new titles. I soon found myself periodically checking the tracking sheets every month, reviewing events that fit my schedule, and setting new goals as we progressed. For me, this energy began flowing right into setting new career goals and establishing manageable steps to achieve them. Of course, this doesn't happen overnight, and achieving goals does take some planning.

Planning

The beginner levels in agility have fewer requirements and simpler, introductory courses to complete to earn titles. While some teams have trouble out of the gate (pun intended) with the beginning levels, it is also not uncommon to experience rapid success at the beginner levels, depending on the team members' preparation and skill level. I have seen some teams begin competing with great success at the beginner levels, then move into the next level and struggle because things suddenly get harder. You can earn a beginner title in as little as two days of competing, so it can happen quickly. Despite our initial challenges, once we started clicking, Heidi and I were one of those teams that moved up before we should have. There is a reason that the Open/Intermediate levels are colloquially referred to as "purgatory." Your training and skills sometimes only get you so far before you realize gaps in your preparation and training.

When I started in dog agility, I assumed everyone had the same goal of earning a qualifying score. As I spent more time in the sport, however, I realized that everyone's goals varied significantly. For some teams, it's all about earning qualifying scores in the events they enter and compete in. They are there to qualify in every run possible and hopefully earn first-place finishes and top honors in the trial. Other teams are coming to play just one game with their dog because they need that one particular qualifying run to earn a specific title. Some teams are competing locally to earn a slot to compete at a higher level at regional and national competitions. And then there are teams like Heidi and me that never competed outside of our local competitions and valued every hard-earned local Q we got!

As a new agility competitor, I was surprised to learn that some teams enter a local trial and willingly forfeit a qualifying run to address a specific training issue they are trying to resolve for future success, focusing only on particular skills in the ring. I have seen top-level competitors stop their dog mid-run, pick it up, and carry it off the course (this is often referred to as the "walk of shame" for the dog). Some dogs never make it past the start line if their handler is training to reinforce a start-line stay, and the dog breaks their stay (an advanced skill). They may have entered "for exhibition only" (FEO) or are choosing to give up a qualifying run, and sometimes, as an observer, you're not sure what happened. It is possible that the dog has not met its training criteria, either by not following a cue from the handler or by engaging in undesired behavior with one of the contact obstacles, and the handler is working to reinforce the expected behavior. Or it may be that the dog is exhibiting signs of an injury, and the handler is concerned about its health. For those teams, a qualifying run isn't their current goal. Instead, long-term health, proper performance, understanding cues and connections, and meeting performance criteria may be their goals for a much longer window of success.

Agility also offers placements based on qualifying scores. First, second, and third place finishers always receive ribbons, and occasionally, at some trials, fourth place is also awarded a ribbon. Qualifying runs are necessary to earn titles at local competitions, and way more than three or four dogs can qualify in a run. Placements are like the icing on the cake of an outstanding performance! They can be crucial at national competitions, as the top dogs are the ones to move on, and the competition for placements is tight at the popular dog jump heights of twelve, sixteen, and twenty inches. As you become more adept as a team, your goal could change from just qualifying to earning first place in your jump height. This may look like a different run than a team looking for a clean qualifying run.

The more I participated, the more I learned that setting goals in dog agility isn't as apparent as you might think, nor is it always evident to observers. Similarly, your goals in work and life may not be as obvious or evident to casual observers. Try not to be unduly swayed or influenced by others, especially those who are not qualified to weigh in.

Always keep in mind that your goals are yours alone. You can learn from others' goals, but do not let them negatively impact your own.

My goals in agility with Heidi were typical. When we started competing, getting qualifying runs was my primary goal for every competition. I closely studied and followed the title chart, beginning at a teacup agility trial close to home, where we worked hard through our beginner, intermediate, and superior levels, earning many titles in standard runs and games. We then worked toward our Teacup Agility Championship title, also known as TACh, earning our first in March 2017.

Throughout her career, Heidi achieved this goal twice. As she aged, however, she began running too slowly to qualify in teacup agility; the course times were too short for her to meet the qualification standards. We were consistently over the standard course time by just a couple of seconds. Achieving the goal of earning qualifying runs and new titles became increasingly rare. Although we had earned a champion title twice in the venue, it became frustrating for both of us. I wasn't willing to accept that she was too old for agility at just eight years old. Something needed to change, and we both needed a new spark.

Before I considered retiring Heidi, I researched different dog agility venues and set some new goals. We started over at the beginning in a different venue and enjoyed quick success due to our team's experience and expertise. It turns out she wasn't too old; we just needed to change our approach. At the Canine Performance Events (CPE) agility venue, which features full-sized equipment and courses, she and I rediscovered the motivation and joy we had experienced in our earlier competitions. Heidi ran like the wind on the big, wide-open courses! Despite facing challenges such as the pandemic and health issues, she earned her Level 2, 3, and 5 titles and achieved her championship (CS-ATCH) in just a few years. She was also just a few qualifying runs short of her second CPE championship (Heidi had thirty-three qualifying runs out of forty required) when she became paralyzed due to the genetic intervertebral disc disease (IVDD). We would have missed many fun years of competing together if I had not adjusted my goals.

Opportunity

Working within the framework of all canine sports has broadened my horizons in setting goals in other areas of my life. The best news is that this process can be applied to both personal goals and professional achievements. If you're an employee, your annual reviews and employer expectations can be used to frame how you can reach your goals that you would like to achieve as an employee. Perhaps it involves being named a partner or shareholder, or assuming an additional level of responsibility and a new title, which hopefully comes with an increased paycheck. If you are an entrepreneur, your business plan should help you establish the framework for setting the goals that you want to achieve, including the massive ones that seem scary and unattainable when you're starting. And if you are dreaming of a new career, this same process can help you meet all the qualifications listed in the job description so you can be ready to make the move. This same process can be applied to promotions, acquiring new clients, exploring new career opportunities, and even submitting for professional recognitions. Setting goals creates boundless growth opportunities.

When I taught business practices to interior designers at a local university, I always included a discussion about networking, which is a vital component for building your professional network and can be improved by setting some basic goals. Now I can't help but see the comparison between agility events and networking events. All competitors enter the same agility event, just like networking event attendees, yet everyone comes to the event with different goals.

There are numerous networking opportunities every month. To achieve the most success in reaching your networking goals, be selective in the events you attend, and consider your motivations and what you intend to gain from them ahead of time. For instance, attending a networking event to meet ten new people with whom you could potentially do business is quite different from someone who has decided to target one person they would like to get an introduction to. With some networking groups, friends who haven't seen each other in a while can get together and socialize. So, if you don't set a goal ahead of time, you can get caught up in socializing and miss that big introduction you were hoping for, or miss opportunities to meet new potential collaborators for work in the future.

Using a framework like the one established in sports, such as agility, and applying it elsewhere can be extremely helpful. We can set those big, hairy, audacious goals (which I equate to a championship title in agility) and then break them down into sub-levels that are more easily achievable. Under these sublevels, we create micro steps that we know are achievable to reach those goals, while considering the roadblocks that we may encounter ahead. Setting goals will help you plan the required training and preparation. It would be amazing if that roadmap came printed out for all of us, like it does in dog agility. But the work is up to us. We must first think through and create our entries to personalize the steps required to achieve the goals we most desire.

Setting goals is a fundamental first step toward achieving personal and professional success.

You may be thinking that goal-setting is a waste of time because you'll never achieve your big goal. But consider me. I never dreamed of what I would accomplish with my canine partner, Heidi. She is not the typical agility champion breed, so I (and likely a few others) often underestimated what we might be capable of. Trust me, with my limited athletic ability and training experience, we truly were underdogs. I was not sure I would ever achieve a championship title with Heidi in any agility venue, yet we earned three (almost four) together!

Overcoming those odds to become a winning team motivated me to push my career goals further. After earning a championship agility title with Heidi, I began thinking more ambitiously about the contributions I could make to the interior design industry. I started exploring opportunities outside of my hometown and region. I also took a chance applying for positions on national committees, and after some initial rejections, I successfully earned my first volunteer role. Since assuming my first national committee member role, I have gained momentum to serve on other committees (at least five so far) and worked toward chairing a national committee with over forty volunteers nationwide.

After years of this amazing volunteer experience advocating for my interior design industry, I decided to apply for national awards. I was hopeful but had no expectations. My fear of failure was largely alleviated after years of participating in agility competitions, and you can't win if you don't apply. I had mixed success the first year, so I reapplied after hearing "no." As I had learned, not every run will be a Q, no matter how badly you might want it! I am proud to share that, after being initially rejected, I was recently named to the American Society of Interior Designers (ASID) College of Fellows, the highest distinction for the top one percent of ASID members, as selected by peer review. That is like winning an agility championship for my interior design career!

I can attest that grit and determination, along with a focus on recording and tracking (sometimes obsessively) for goal achievement, helped us achieve more than I ever thought possible. It is also important to remember that self-advocacy may be critical to your success, especially if you feel like an underdog. You may think, "I'll never achieve that goal in a million years." Well, if you don't believe you can, you probably won't. But if you try and set some steps toward reaching that goal, what's the worst thing that can happen? Maybe you don't ever reach that big, hairy, audacious goal. I will never achieve a second CPE championship title alongside Heidi due to her career-ending injury. But together we accomplished more than I ever thought possible! I never dreamed I could be named an ASID Fellow, but by setting goals, working hard, and accepting help along the way, it became a reality. You may not reach the biggest goal you set, but you will accomplish a great deal along the way. And I also want to stress that, as important as goals are, don't forget to enjoy the journey, not just the result.

Photo Credit: Virginia Weida

Winning Goals Strategies:
- **Set SMART goals (Specific, Measurable, Achievable, Relevant, Time-Based).**
- **List actionable items.**
- **Plan ahead, measure progress, and adapt.**
- **Enjoy the journey, not just the outcome.**

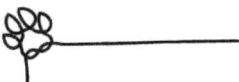

HEIDI'S PAWS FOR THOUGHT:

Never underestimate what you are capable of.

Chapter Three - Mentality

Heidi would never encourage someone to practice more than was necessary. She has such natural talent that she only needs to try things a few times before she has one-hundred-percent confidence that she can do it. Whenever we would do the same sequence in an agility class, by the second or third pass, she would slow down and stop running or leave me altogether to sniff around the perimeter of the room (a favorite hound-dog activity). She found practice incredibly dull, but I needed practice to gain my confidence. Heidi would push my limits to find creative ways to practice while keeping it fun and enjoyable for her. As my confidence increased, so did my optimism for our team's success and desire to compete more. These are some of the stepping stones to mentality, and Heidi was a great coach.

Remember: In life, attitude is everything.

Competing in dog agility was totally outside of my comfort zone. I had few of the core abilities, naturally, while my partner, Heidi, had many. But the more I learned about it, the more I wanted to try it. I took that first leap of faith, and I am grateful every day for finding that courage. Really, what did I have to lose if we failed, except a couple of dollars and some pride? The leap came with low personal risk, and I believed that we could do it.

I experienced similar doubts when starting my entrepreneurial journey, although admittedly, my risk felt much higher since it was my career and not a hobby. Although I wasn't an expert in business ownership, I had fourteen years of experience in interior design and project management. I felt significantly more qualified when I started my own company in 2006 than I did for my first agility competition in 2013!

It is impossible to know everything. A positive attitude, combined with a dash of courage, can help you take the first step toward a new goal.

Bold optimism and a growth mindset give you the edge to achieve success and win. These qualities give you the strength to overcome obstacles, the confidence to grow, the belief that abilities can improve with effort, and the resilience to take risks. It all begins with a positive outlook.

Shoot for the Moon

Optimism is both simple and complicated at the same time. Optimism is having a positive outlook and the belief that you can accomplish something, even in the absence of proof. Optimism in dog agility means stepping to the line with your canine partner and believing that you can complete the course together and earn a qualifying run. Your very first run of your first trial requires an extraordinary dose of optimism just to enter and show up. You have little to no evidence that you and your canine partner will succeed together, yet you still sign up.

I'm speaking from experience. My first agility trial with Heidi did not go as I had hoped. Heidi had an absolute blast! I was actually surprised by the outcome. Although I expected it would go better than it did, the overall experience was about so much more than the results. I realized that I had much more to learn, but I also believed that success would eventually come. If I had been totally overwhelmed, we would have moved on to try something else. You should always follow your instincts about those types of things. But I was optimistic that we would improve enough to compete. Personally, I love a challenge.

When you enter a trial or competition, the other handlers will tell you, "Have fun with your dog. The dog did not send in the entry form." Dogs, as a species, appear to be naturally optimistic. It takes little prompting for them to be excited about their favorite activities (just think about how often you have to spell W-A-L-K around them). Even if something negative happens, they generally remain optimistic that the next time around, it will be better.

Dogs are always looking for signs that something good is about to happen, and they are fully present to support and encourage it. Whenever a dog hears a wrapper crinkling, they show up for a treat and beg until they get one. Whenever you put on your shoes and grab your car keys, they are ready to go for a ride and will whine and fuss until you take them. Whenever you make dinner and sit down at the table, they are under your feet begging for a bite, or at least hoping to snag a stray crumb that drops to the floor.

This routine repeats itself every time the signs are present, regardless of whether something good happened the last time or not. Crinkling wrappers, jingling car keys, and plates being taken out of the cupboard must mean something good is about to happen! They are persistently optimistic. Consider for a moment how you approach your daily routine. Is it with a sense of wonder and excitement about the good things to come, or with dread that something might go wrong? Which way leads to more success and fulfillment?

It could be dogs' natural optimism that encourages us to keep trying new things. Although I didn't have a great first trial with Heidi, I remained optimistic that we could do better the next time. It took us more than a few attempts to find success and earn a qualifying score. And when we did, it felt so good! Even today, after participating in agility for more than ten years, when I look at a course map that includes challenges beyond my current team's capability, I'm still optimistic that it could work out. And if it doesn't, I will still have learned some new skills our team needs to practice.

An optimistic outlook leads to greater overall mental strength and confidence.

I must have an ingrained "the cup is half full" mentality. If you believe the outcome will be favorable, your confidence will be higher. On the other hand, when you let your doubts creep in, you can talk yourself into a negative result. Preparation also helps your confidence while simultaneously building your optimism. Both work together to bring you greater success. When I have a day where the agility courses are not in my favor, I still believe in our team and that we can get it next time. Although at first, you may not have any proof that it will necessarily happen, that outlook will lead you to success more quickly. Competing in a sport like agility is a great way to conquer the fear of failure!

Optimism also drives participation. If you believe you can do it, and you believe that you have a chance at being successful, you are more than likely to complete that entry, make that phone call, send in that job application, apply for that promotion, or create that business entity. Optimism is not something you can study or buy, but it is something that you can practice and develop. There is a quote that I often hear: "Shoot for the moon, and you will land among the stars." I encourage you to take that chance and be optimistic that it will work out. More often than not, it works out in your favor, whether you can see it at the time or not.

Resilience

Resilience is well expressed in the Japanese proverb about standing up one more time than you fall. It is moving forward in the face of adversity, pushing aside the fear of failure, and overcoming obstacles that may be in the way. We have reviewed persistence, perseverance, and passion, all of which are related to building resiliency. Embracing resiliency takes practice and resolve. Often, it's the kind of practice that doesn't come from a gym and requires mental practice.

We can look to our canine partners for incredible examples of resilience. Heidi suffered a career-ending disc issue in her spine caused by IVDD when she was almost twelve years old in 2023. IVDD is a genetic condition, so there was no traumatic incident or situation, but rather the quietest of injuries. She simply could not stand up, whereas moments before, she had been walking normally. She came home within a day of having emergency back surgery, where they removed two ruptured discs, and began her long road to recovery.

To be honest, Heidi handled it the best out of all of us—humans and canines alike! She seemed to take her situation in stride and demonstrated incredible resilience with a strong recovery. The neurology team referred to her as stoic because, during her time with them, she did not display any discomfort, fear, or any of the typical reactions that would naturally occur in such situations. My husband and I were overcome with worry and concern about her recovery, imagining all the possible outcomes while following our new strict routine, administering countless medications, and constantly keeping her safe and comfortable. The rest of the pack, our three other dogs, were concerned about the changes in Heidi and initially seemed restless and untethered. They were lost without their leader. But Heidi seemed to take everything in stride, enjoying her time in her private recovery crates and managing to rule the pack somehow, even while being confined. She has formidable mental fortitude.

Heidi taught me the power of being resilient and learning to take things in stride.

Today, Heidi has regained approximately ninety percent of her mobility and lives a full life, even though her agility career came to a swift and sudden end. She had a long recovery, physically, while my recovery was more mental. A significant difference between us and our canine partners is that we humans anticipate and worry about all the potential problems that could arise. In contrast, our partners live in the moment. We needlessly expend so much energy!

It is impossible to set aside all worry. In fact, a bit of worry helps keep me on track in all areas of my life. I feel equally about nerves before an agility run or a work presentation. Both keep me focused and serve as a reminder of how much I care about what I'm doing. In my career, resilience means heading back to the job site after a tough meeting and pushing the project forward despite the challenges ahead. It means leading the committee to find a solution when plans go sideways. It means examining your core expertise and finding the courage to explore new avenues for business when work slows down, projects wrap up, or clients move on. Nelson Mandela once said, "I never lose. I either win or learn." This statement reflects a resilient mindset. It is possible to become more optimistic and resilient through confidence, which we most often build with proper practice and preparation.

Be Prepared!

Preparation helps immeasurably with setting and achieving goals. Not only does it allow for greater flexibility, but it also fuels resilience when things don't go as planned. Preparation can be mental, emotional, and physical, encompassing both internal and external components. As a dog handler for canine sports, the preparation for both team members falls squarely on the human.

At your first agility trial, you may only think about bringing things to take care of the dog and forget about taking care of yourself. Most new handlers will bring a dog bowl for water, some treats, a poop bag or two, and a leash. That is enough to get you through a walk in the park; however, competitions are much more involved. If you are at a competition for any length of time, you will need dog food and bowls, training treats, a crate for the dog, and a folding chair for yourself, at a minimum.

Once you get more involved in dog sports, you realize that those initial things are just scratching the surface of what you need. You are often at a site as early as six or seven in the morning and stay there for up to twelve hours some days. Some locations require a mat under your chair and crates, so before long, you begin investing in a nicer, portable chair, an indoor/outdoor rug, collapsible water and food bowls, and a new collapsible dog crate with comfy mats inside. The list is endless.

And what about supplies for the human half of the team? You'll soon realize the importance of bringing a spare pair of tennis shoes. At most venues, stepping into mud or a puddle outside means you can no longer wear your shoes on the indoor running surface. Many handlers also keep a spare change of clothing in case of spills or falls, as well as some snacks and a packed lunch. As you become even more involved in the sport, your list of essentials expands, particularly if you are staying overnight in a hotel.

The preparation I did for canine sports helped me become better prepared for my work days. Similar to my dog excursion days, at work I always have a spare bottle of water and some non-perishable snacks in my bag. I carry an extra pen or two and a spare set of batteries for my electronic devices, as well as charging cables and connectors. Small first-aid kits are also great to keep close by.

Beyond the supplies, there are essential tasks I do to prepare for work. One example is mapping out the route before meeting with a new client or visiting a new job site. With the tools we have today, there's no reason not to research the company, the person you're meeting with, and the address to get a visual of the building or location you're going to. You can check the parking situation and be better prepared to know if you need to have cash (or even coins) to pay for parking. To prepare effectively for any activity, set clear goals for what you want to accomplish, have a contingency plan in case things don't go as planned, and stay organized. Keep critical information together, with both a paper and an electronic backup copy available.

Preparation is vital to consider for yourself, your work tools, your travel to and from different locations, and preparing for others, if applicable. Being prepared enables us to focus on the task at hand and stay more present in the moment. It's impossible to prepare for every outcome, but if you run through a fair number of scenarios, you will be better off than if you don't prepare anything at all. Preparation lays the groundwork for success. It reduces anxiety and boosts your confidence, enabling you to anticipate and react to challenges more effectively. When you practice and prepare sufficiently, day-to-day tasks become muscle memory, which frees your mind to allow for greater flexibility and creative problem-solving in the heat of the moment.

~~Practice~~ Confidence

When I was drafting this book, one of the original winning bitch traits on my list was "Practice." I needed lots of practice to compete in agility, or any dog sport for that matter. Practice improves my skills and builds my confidence. Music and theater productions I participated in as a youth required a lot of practice, so I am accustomed to the routine. I also come from a long line of teachers, and I love to learn new things. But if I'm genuinely thinking about this from Heidi's perspective, she would one-hundred-percent say (if she could speak, that is) that practice is stupid and overrated, and that confidence is much more critical. We cover some basics of practice in more detail in the chapter on training. Until then, we will focus more on how practice plays a role in building confidence.

If you have performed a specific job or procedure repeatedly, then perhaps the idea of practice isn't the best motivator for you either. Suppose, however, that you are new to your industry or position, or that you're considering a significant change. In that case, I believe practice is an incredibly valuable exercise for building confidence, since confidence can be a massive differentiating factor in your success. Practice and confidence build upon one another—the more your confidence grows through practice, the more confidently you practice.

The right kind of practice leads to confidence.

Simply doing more repetitions of something is not necessarily better; targeted practice is often more effective. Heidi never allowed me unlimited reps. Just once or twice on a course was all she would tolerate, so I had to make it count. Heidi mastered her agility maneuvers and was much more adept overall than I was at mastering my handling skills. She straight-up never required as much practice as I did. And Heidi absolutely approaches every situation with confidence, whether or not she has done it before. We could all use a confidence boost like that in our work and life!

Even though you have experience and skills, do you approach a new situation thinking *I'm in over my head, I don't have anything valuable to add to this conversation,* or *I have no idea what I am doing here*? If so, you may be struggling with a version of imposter syndrome, where you doubt your skills and abilities. Women are often less likely than men to feel capable of applying for new positions, even if they possess as many as seven out of ten skills, whereas men think they are capable if they have just a few skills. Self-doubt can kill confidence and negatively impact your success.

In work and life, we may rely on others for our confidence, which can be even trickier. In a close partnership like agility, your emotional states can influence each other. The handler's feelings travel down the leash to the dog. Similarly, the dog's feelings can travel back up the leash to the handler. If a handler steps to the start line and their mindset is that they are underqualified, in over their head, or that the course is just impossible, the likelihood is that they will not be successful. Sometimes, the dog tells us they are anxious or overstimulated when we step to the start line, and the run may fall apart. The reverse can also occur, where the calm, confident handler can soothe the dog, and the confident dog can calm the handler. Dogs offer us unconditional love and support, and our connection can enable us to support each other's needs.

A big part of confidence is the old adage to "never let them see you sweat." You might be panicked on the inside, but if you present yourself calmly on the outside, no one may know. As a woman working in commercial real estate, there have been moments in my career when I have been in a room and briefly wondered how I got there. But I would never let that insecurity show. The "fake it till you make it" approach to winning at work was not always successful in agility, however, because our canine partners are much more perceptive than our human counterparts. Our pets are highly attuned to our physiological states. If you are feeling turmoil on the inside, your heart rate has likely increased, your breathing rate has changed, and you may even be emitting an odor that dogs can interpret as fear. I had to work even harder on building my confidence in new situations, which benefited me greatly in the long run.

Take a chance on yourself.

Confidence doesn't happen overnight, and you may have doubts about stepping out of your comfort zone. I highly encourage you to take that first step. I'm proof that you can learn to do different things and even excel! In my office closet, I now have bins full of dog awards. This is a massive contrast to my life before canine sports, where I had only earned a five-inch-high trophy for being in the band in elementary school. I don't compete for the ribbons, but they are physical reminders of our successful journey together. I earned many of these through competing with Heidi, as well as with my older female partner, Penny, and now my new younger male partner, Gus Gus. These canine sports are pretty athletic, and you already know that I was a band member, not an athlete. Granted, I am not a top world agility competitor, nor do I aspire to be one, but we are continuously training and competing locally and having a grand time.

Practice will help you build confidence, and as you have some success, your concerns about being an impostor will naturally diminish. There are also confidence exercises you can practice, which focus on posture, expression, vocal control, and projection. For example, years ago I was attending a presentation with a room full of women. The speaker had us stand up and practice the "Wonder Woman" classic pose— straight back, chin up, feet planted, and hands on hips. You get the idea. She suggested we do that strength pose as a confidence booster before anything we had to do that we were nervous about. Go ahead and give it a try—it works!

When I worked with college students and women returning to the workforce, we reviewed the concept of "personal power." One aspect of this concept is the importance of appearing professional and how body language can convey confidence, even when you don't feel it. Just like the Wonder Woman pose, we can practice improving our posture, facial expressions, and walking confidently in front of a mirror. Good posture naturally makes you take up more space and appear more confident. We also need to watch our arm position so that we don't appear defensive or nervous. For example, crossing your arms gives the impression that you are unapproachable or closed off. Making eye contact and smiling can also help you project confidence (even if you might not feel it yet).

Confidence can help us win by:

- Inspiring trust.
- Reinforcing credibility.
- Building new relationships.
- Pursuing innovation.
- Strengthening leadership.

Having confidence helps you build resilience and gives you the courage to take greater risks. It also helps you stand out from the crowd. These risks don't have to be big or reckless. They can include things like making decisions without having all the answers, entering competitions, or submitting a job application without mastering every skill. Simply participating will help alleviate the overall fear of failure that we all share. Accepting that trying something new may not work out will bring you greater success than not trying anything at all.

Preparation involves mentally and physically getting ready to accomplish the goals that you have set out to achieve. Preparation leads to greater confidence, but confidence is also a significant mental game-changer in its own right. We have all met people who should be confident but are not, and people who should not be confident but are overly so. Optimism is also a mental activity that requires switching from a doom-and-gloom mindset to a more positive outlook. Resiliency can be physical, but it requires mental strength to be willing to come back, push through, or start over, depending on the situation. Heidi is incredibly resilient, hopeful, and optimistic. She is seemingly naturally prepared with minimal effort, and she's outrageously confident. These qualities embody mental strength and the importance of mentality in winning. She was a great coach for these qualities, and I soaked it all in.

Photo Credit: Virginia Weida

Winning Mentality Strategies:
- **Take the first step.**
- **Embrace optimism without evidence.**
- **Never lose.**
- **Be outrageously confident.**

HEIDI'S PAWS FOR THOUGHT:

Practice is overrated.
Be confident.

Chapter Four - Training

Heidi was naturally athletic. She was a fast learner, and she never struggled with any of the required elements in agility. Some dogs have issues with tunnels because of the darkness. Not Heidi. She was a tunnel sucker and would dive right in, always hoping to find a badger inside. Some dogs dislike the teeter because it moves; Heidi wanted it to be higher and fall faster. Some dogs are tentative on the A-frame; Heidi felt like she was on top of the world. She could also run really, really fast.

Conversely, in the beginning, I was totally out of my element. Though I didn't need to learn to perform the obstacles (that's just for the dogs), I did have to run the courses. The most athletic thing I've ever done was participating in high school marching band! But to win, Heidi and I needed each other. I initially required significantly more training than she did, and naturally, she was a bit impatient with me. Heidi wanted to win, and I was holding her back. Let the training begin!

In dog sports, training is crucial for success. You are embarking on an adventure with a species that's wholly different from your own. You are not riding them, nor are you leashed to them for direction. You have to connect with your partner in other ways to succeed. Agility training can be broad, especially for beginners. It can also become hyper-focused on a particular issue that your team faces. This could be establishing performance criteria for the contact obstacles, like the dog walk or the A-frame. It could be working through fear on the teeter. It could be focusing on a tendency to drop or knock bars down. Or it could be helping your dog become more reliable in performing the weave poles. Other things that training can help your dog with include being comfortable in a new location, ignoring distractions in the ring, refraining from interacting with dogs outside the ring while running your turn, and learning to stay with your handler instead of sniffing along the fence or visiting ring workers during your run. These are all situations we had to train for at one time or another.

Strong foundations are essential, and inherent talent can both aid and hinder your success.

I trained to compensate for my innate agility limitations so Heidi and I could compete together as a team. However, training is not limited to athletic pursuits only. Learning is a key trait for success in many aspects of life, whether you have continuing education requirements in your career or not. While my journey with Heidi has enhanced my skills for my career in commercial real estate, the training regimen that I follow to be a better handler for my canine partners is mirrored in my professional life. If you are working toward a career change, whether it involves a promotion, transitioning to a new industry, or starting your own venture, establishing core competencies is critical to that endeavor. Innate abilities may only get you so far. Uncovering what we need to know is a gift, but we must also be willing to identify our shortfalls and train for improved outcomes.

Training, or continuous learning, is one of the most effective ways I have found to achieve competitive excellence. It polishes skills, refreshes our industry knowledge, allows us to level up, and gives us that edge to win. Training demands a structured approach, including familiarization to establish a strong foundation, targeted practice, and real-world application. We learn the most by doing. Successful training strategies also involve engaging coaches, seeking out mentors, and learning from multiple sources. It is not a solo endeavor. I encourage you to consider training in a new way to enhance your skills and lay a solid foundation for success.

Skill Development

Early training in agility means establishing core competencies. Initially, you may believe that because you have a dog that likes to run fast, your team can simply drop in and excel at agility. True, running fast is a valuable core competency, but other critical skills need to be developed. Whenever we set out to try something new, we need to create a basic toolkit of skills. This learning process is similar for every new venture, from the basics we learned in kindergarten to the specialized training required for our careers. A significant part of starting something new involves learning the vocabulary specific to that activity. The more we read, listen to podcasts, attend classes, study, train, and engage in these activities, the more we become familiar with the lingo. This rings true for work, hobbies, and especially activities like dog sports. You need to learn the building blocks to build a strong foundation, which will help you continue to grow.

Core competencies in agility are usually covered in your first training class. These include basics such as recognizing what an agility jump is and how to do it safely. Just like you learn to ride a bike with training wheels, jumps are often set at low levels in the beginning to ease dogs into it. You'd think going through a tunnel would be a simple thing for a dog to do. But from a dog's perspective, tunnels are often black holes, and when they are curved, they cannot see the way out, so they hesitate about going in. Some great agility dogs struggle with the tunnel in the beginning. So, we break it down in training and offer lots of treats and encouragement to help them learn tunnels.

In a beginner class, dogs learn how to walk a narrow plank flat on the floor. This helps them get comfortable on a narrow plank (to mimic a dog walk safely) when it is raised off the floor. These classes also feature wobble boards, which are wooden discs with a rounded, bowl-shaped pivot on the bottom, allowing the board to tilt when dogs place their paws on it. Motion is another competency that dogs need to become comfortable with so they can eventually execute the teeter safely.

Heidi loved the early training classes, and her core competencies pointed to future success. She was super fast (even with her short legs), a quick learner, and fearless. During our first training session, she watched the instructor with the demo dog and then did the behavior on her own immediately to earn a reward! However, the same core competencies that pointed to success would also pose challenges down the road. On the positive side, being super fast enables a dog to do the course quickly as numbered. On the flip side, it may leave the handler in the dust, as the dog does circles around the ring with the breeze in its hair and not a care in the world. Yes, I speak from experience—this has happened to me a few too many times to count!

Building core competencies in a sport like dog agility parallels the learning process that occurs when you start a new career, take on a new position after a promotion, or launch a new company. Working for a larger company in your industry is valuable, as it provides expertise in developing core skills and gaining experience. While experience and inherent talent may enable you to succeed initially, it's not necessarily indicative of thriving long-term without some additional knowledge and training.

Practice

When I first started competing in canine sports, I believed that one class a week would be sufficient. (Spoiler alert: I was utterly mistaken!) During the week, we would practice new skills outside of class for a few minutes here and there, but we primarily came to our classes to work and learn. I relied heavily on Heidi's skills without realizing my shortcomings. After gaining some experience, it became clear that attending class once a week was not enough to improve our team's skills, particularly if we were remotely interested in competing in any venue. The more I learned, the more I realized I didn't know.

Practice doesn't just mean doing the same thing repeatedly, which can become boring and work against you. There are numerous guides to improving your practice skills. One of my favorite hacks is breaking down a larger skill into smaller parts and working on different aspects each time you run through it. Whenever I'm training a dog on new behaviors, and the overall task is too advanced, we work together on the steps one or two at a time, then backchain them together until the dog can complete a whole sequence. It's like learning a dance. A dance team doesn't just start at the beginning and learn a brand-new dance all in one sitting. They work on it bit by bit, sequence by sequence, and then they put the pieces together. As they rerun the sequence, they may focus on arm/hand positions in one take and leg/feet positions in the next. Working with dogs has shown me that the more we repeat the same things, especially in the same order, the more the team becomes accustomed to that pattern.

As an assistant volunteer agility instructor, our class runs a fun exercise for new handlers. They run the same short sequence of a few jumps and a tunnel a couple of times in a row, and then I have them try to run it with a change to a different jump at the end. Most dogs still follow the original sequence instead of what the handler is asking, and they do it with confidence, because that is what they practiced. This is an example of patterning—a behavioral trap that we can fall into when we repeatedly perform a specific sequence of actions. And if a situation causes the order to change suddenly, we may not be able to react fast enough.

With a sport like agility, you want consistent behaviors, especially around the contact obstacles for safety. But the order of behaviors or the pattern is different every time. We are asking for a higher skill than just repeating the performance of things in the same order over and over. With Heidi's personality, she rarely became patterned, because she would not do the same thing over and over, even if I asked. The novelty of a situation kept her engaged and interested. The second things became routine, however, she would do something that she found more rewarding, which was often leaving me to go on a sniffing safari along the fence line. That brought her great joy, of course, and much frustration to me!

My current agility partner, Gus Gus, is a little more amenable to doing repeated practice runs than Heidi was. That said, I have noticed that even he will start to pattern and get bored if we do it repeatedly. Just like people, dogs can go on autopilot when they are stuck in a repetitive task. Honestly, I don't enjoy practice much myself. When I was a child taking piano lessons, I got into loads of trouble because I didn't practice enough. It was likely the repetition of the same thing that I found demotivating and too demanding. When I am learning a new skill or performing a repetitive task, I now give myself enough time to work in breaks so I can do something different in between.

You will get what you practice, both in dog sports and in your work endeavors!

There is a famous quote by the late mystery novelist Rita Mae Brown (not Albert Einstein, as many mistakenly believe): *"Insanity is doing the same thing over and over again and expecting different results."* If you are not satisfied with the results, mixing up your practice and routine is likely to yield a different outcome. To avoid repetition or patterned tasks, try varying the order or switching between tasks. Set SMART goals with microsteps built in. With dogs, you can focus on different aspects, such as mastering a specific handling technique or working on a particular behavior with them each time. I often ran the class agility course with Heidi in reverse on the second turn. I also tried new handling ideas to keep things interesting by not being in the same place on the course at the same time, using different crosses to help her keep her focus.

When it comes to your personal or professional life, it might be helpful to consider practicing differently to keep your interest, too. For example, in my work activities, I have a nice mix of left-brained and right-brained tasks that I always need to complete. If I'm not being productive in one area or another, I switch to a different type of task to avoid boredom and increase productivity.

Are you running on autopilot most of the day? Consider mixing up your tasks or challenging yourself to keep yourself motivated. One skill that anyone can practice is active listening, a form of listening that requires attention and engagement (as opposed to simply considering how to reply to what is being said). Are you focused on business operations and training new employees? Consider varying their learning sessions to prevent them from performing overly repetitive tasks, thereby reducing boredom and enhancing engagement.

Are you focused on marketing? For your client calls, practice your script to become more confident, and ask existing clients for referrals. Another vital marketing aspect to practice is the elevator pitch (i.e., a twenty- to thirty-second response to the question, "So, what do you do?" You will be asked this in both work and personal settings, and the proper response can pique the other person's interest in asking more questions. Sometimes, practicing can be as fundamental as attending networking events that you might find uncomfortable so you can become more comfortable with the process of mingling and introducing yourself to new people.

Practice will not bring perfection, but if done correctly, it will yield stronger results over time.

Practice is fundamental because rehearsals almost always lead to a better performance. Dedication to practice is a critical consideration; we must make time for it. I was running my company, raising my children, and training and competing with Heidi all at the same time, so I didn't have a lot of extra time or resources to dedicate to training and practice. Lucky for us, Heidi learned things quickly and didn't require as much practice as I did. With my current canine partner, most of my ring practice takes place at a facility located approximately an hour away. It is a commitment to our training. The facility is top-notch with fantastic instructors, and I am grateful that it's relatively close by, as there are competitors in other parts of the country that have to drive even further than we do to train and compete. Gratitude can impact your mindset and the outcome of your practice. Shifting from thinking "I have to" to "I get to" can be life-altering.

Keep training fun! Think about it: What are the chances you'll have success teaching a dog a new trick if you offer no reward and speak in a low, monotone voice? More than likely, the dog will quickly move on and find something else that brings them happiness. When I train a dog, I always use positive reinforcement. This includes giving them lots of praise in a happy voice, as well as lots of training treats. I also keep our training sessions shorter to help keep boredom at bay. I never punish the dog when they don't immediately exhibit the behavior I am looking for. Instead, I encourage their positive attempts and keep practicing until we achieve success. This may take anywhere from a few minutes to several months, depending on the nature of the skill. Giving rewards and having a positive attitude will keep training fun for all!

Mentorship

Training used to be very specific to locations and limited to trainers with whom you had in-person access. With the advent of technology, it is now possible to train virtually with coaches worldwide! My team's training involves reading articles and blogs, attending seminars, watching video reviews by coaches, reading books, observing training videos by others, and participating in weekly, hands-on, one-on-one in-person sessions. I also volunteer to teach at our local dog club, where we work with teams that are new to the sport. It's gratifying to see novice teams progress, and teaching the basics helps me stay current with handling methodology. Having access to such a wide range of experts can also help evolve your training from just repeating a skill into something more beneficial for success. There is more than one way to learn a skill, and different experts may offer new training methods. This guidance has been invaluable in helping me understand some of the most complex agility skills.

Throughout my professional life and entrepreneurial journey, the evolution of technology has also provided invaluable access to experts in my field. We are no longer restricted to printed books or magazines, nor are we limited to professionals within our geographic area. We have unlimited access to articles, seminars, training resources, blogs, and social media tools that can connect us to the experts we need for any situation. We can seek out these opportunities, utilize all available resources, and evolve as our experience grows.

Training can also include learning from those around you. Years ago, when Heidi and I were a new team, we attended a judging seminar in a new place to us, where judges-in-training practiced in a mock trial setting. When it was our turn to run, a venerable judge was in the ring, and Heidi did what Heidi did best in those early days, especially in a new place. She put her nose to the ground, did a handful of jumps, and then ran to the perimeter of the ring and sniffed the fence, gating all along the ring. All the while, the clock was ticking; you only have forty to sixty seconds for each run. When I could not get her back after a few seconds, the judge put his hands on his hips and told me sternly that I needed a better recall on my dog. (A recall is a "come when called, despite the stimulus" command that highly trained dogs can do even when something is incredibly interesting to them, such as chasing a deer or other wildlife.) I was wasting his time.

As a newer competitor, I was embarrassed and mortified to be called out for an apparent weakness in our training. But in the moment I recognized that it would not have mattered if I had been a flaming hot steak off the grill. She simply had no interest in what I was asking her to do. Heidi was doing what she wanted to do in the moment and was following her innate traits for her breed. Dachshunds can be incredibly impulsive and determined at times. It was not an excuse, but rather an understanding of my partner and her motivations. Many years of training helped us achieve eventual success, despite her hound dog characteristics. But in that moment, I felt totally defeated.

Eventually, I managed to collect Heidi from the ring and return to my chair, where I felt humiliated and sorry for myself. I was still new to the sport and did not know many people. A few moments later, a woman approached me and said, "Thank you." To which I was thinking, *What for?* In my mind, I hadn't done anything but embarrass myself and my team. She quickly added that she had been experiencing some frustration while training her mixed-breed dog. It had some dachshund in its genetic makeup, but her trainers had not worked with that breed much before. They all believed that her dog was being willful and disinterested in training, no matter what she had tried, when in fact, the dog may have been exhibiting innate breed behaviors that appeared as disinterest.

This was a light-bulb moment for her, as she realized that she would need to consider ways to train around and redirect that behavior, rather than try to change it. She learned from our run in the ring that her dog may not be specifically disinterested in agility training, but rather that its innate behaviors were more rewarding in that moment than what the human partner was asking for. Of course, helping someone else strengthen their relationship with their dog made me feel a little better about my disastrous run. That experience definitely gave me a list of things to continue training on.

It is vital to have a feedback loop to grow from experience, including self-evaluation, expert reviews, and learning from others.

In agility, the best competitors watch other teams run a course in a competition so they can cement their plan, learn something they may have missed when they walked through the course, or see a handling maneuver that they want to consider. What is your feedback loop for your professional work? If you are employed by others, it may be the annual review. As an entrepreneur, your ability to earn referrals may be limited if you don't ask for client feedback or reviews. But don't forget to watch other competitors. Follow their social media, cheer their success, and use that to help generate new ideas and learn from them. Remember that training can be both broad and hyper-focused, both of which can help you create greater opportunities. Be open to new ideas and new sources of information!

This dedication to training with my dogs has improved my approach to other aspects of my life. The benefits may be more noticeable in agility, as you visibly see improved performance of your team, both while training and in competitions. It may take longer to see the benefits in your professional life. Still, I have learned that training improves competence, builds confidence in navigating new situations, and reduces the fear of failure. Training brings you to new levels of success through expanded knowledge and expertise, and your decision-making skills improve as you gain experience, allowing you to adapt and remain flexible. Training is fundamental for achieving our goals in all areas of life, enabling us to grow and set new objectives to strive for.

Continuous Learning

I have never met a more motivated group of individuals dedicated to continuous learning than those I have encountered while competing in dog sports. They are so invested in gaining knowledge for its own sake. They are not striving to achieve degrees or certifications; they recognize that the learning process is ongoing and infinite. Even the best competitors constantly train and learn. Whether your field of work requires continuing education credits or not, I highly encourage you to seek out opportunities for professional development.

Continuing education is a requirement in occupations that require licenses, such as most medical fields, professions like architecture and engineering, building construction trades, real estate, education, and, yes, interior design. This requirement is necessary because, regardless of the field, discoveries are being made, and experience (often tragedies) necessitates updating relevant standards and procedures. Ways to expand your knowledge (if continuous learning is not part of your routine yet) include attending a seminar or conference on a topic that interests you, finding podcasts or blogs by entertainers or experts that you find engaging, or following content creators on social media. Be open to learning opportunities! This thirst for knowledge can provide a broader range of conversation topics, spark a new hobby, or even lead to a career change.

You can learn things solely for the information gained, or you can work toward a new accreditation, often displayed by the alphabet soup after someone's name. I have earned four professional credentials to demonstrate my expertise in the field of commercial interior design. None of them is required; they are all voluntary, and I completed them over the course of three decades. To maintain my credentials after testing, I am required to fulfill continuing education requirements within a specified timeframe. To maintain these certifications, I am responsible for identifying courses, completing the required coursework, tracking progress, and submitting reports to the relevant agencies for credit. I have created specialized spreadsheets to help me stay on track. This takes time and dedication, and contributes to my professional development and success. This process for earning and maintaining professional certifications has guided my approach to training for canine sports. I continually seek out learning opportunities and have spreadsheets that help me track my progress for each venue, as they all have different requirements. I also have to reconcile records continually.

The lessons learned from training a dog in agility— recognizing that practice is a key to improvement, knowing when to ask for help, and understanding that even the greatest have coaches—can apply to other parts of life. Everyone has skills that they can work on, even those who have been in their career for a while. People often mistakenly believe they have to do everything themselves. They miss the opportunity to bring in a coach for areas in which they need improvement, to review their performance, to identify areas for improvement, and to keep them current with literature and podcasts related to their area of expertise. Training is time-consuming and resource-intensive, requiring significant effort. However, the benefits are incomparable for your success.

Photo Credit: Life's Memories Photos by Lisa Urbassik

Winning Training Strategies:
- **Honestly assess shortfalls.**
- **Build strong foundations.**
- **Seek feedback and mentorship.**
- **Embrace lifelong learning.**

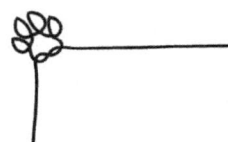

HEIDI'S PAWS FOR THOUGHT:

Showcase your innate ability.

Chapter Five - Adaptability

Since the day we brought her home, Heidi has always kept me on my toes. She was quite an active puppy and required constant supervision and attention. When we began competing in sports, I quickly learned to expect the unexpected. I would go left; she would go right. I would cue a tunnel; she would take an A-frame. I would turn to the center of the ring; she would run to the outside to sniff and explore. We trialed at one venue that had a storage room with a curtain along the wall inside the ring. The curtain was enough of a barrier for every dog except my little one, who could easily slip underneath to explore. I came to expect that behavior during our runs there (as did everyone else, who thoroughly enjoyed her antics!) and tried to anticipate it with better handling.

Through practice, training, and a better understanding of her non-verbal communication, I became much more adept at reacting to new situations on the fly. Heidi gave me a masterclass on becoming more flexible, enabling me to find creative solutions and grow my confidence. The journey had its ups and downs, but not outs. It was challenging to master these skills that were critical for growth.

An adaptable mindset and the ability to quickly change gears are skills both forged and honed in dog agility. In most agility venues, you have standard runs, which always consist of a numbered course and include a variety of jumps, tunnels, weave poles, and contact obstacles. The length of the course and the number of contacts can vary from beginner to higher levels. Additionally, some venues offer agility games that incorporate concepts from a standard course but have distinct rules for each game. The three venues I am most familiar with differ in the games offered. In American Kennel Club (AKC) Agility, two games may be offered at trials, in addition to the standard and jumpers runs. In Canine Performance Events Agility (CPE), there are six games that the judge can select from for each trial in addition to the standard course. And in the Teacup Dog Agility Association (TDAA) venue, there are literally hundreds of games the judges can choose from for each trial.

There is a common game in CPE dog agility and TDAA, among others, that competitors seem to either love or hate; few competitors are ambivalent about it. The game is called Snooker, and it has some complex rules. It can seem complicated, especially in the moment, and can easily confuse new handlers. Unlike a standard course, where you run obstacles in order from one through sixteen or more, the game of Snooker is a two-part game. It has an opening and a closing series. The closing series is similar to a standard agility run, where specific obstacles must be completed in a numbered course, following the proper numerical order and direction, which can be tricky. The numbered closing always starts at two and goes to seven. Your team must complete these six final numbered obstacles accurately, meaning they must not knock or drop any bars, complete the weave poles if included, and perform any contacts, such as the teeter and A-frame, according to standard safety practices.

The fun part of this game (or the part many handlers find most challenging) is the opening part of Snooker. The opening series is a course that you, as a handler, must make up to meet the game's requirements, and it has specific rules. Four red, single-bar jumps are part of every snooker course. Three are required to be used in your opening sequence, with a numbered point obstacle in between; one is a bonus (or a distraction, depending on the situation). The handler's job is to map out a course that suits their canine partner, earns the necessary points, and achieves their overall goal. The game is scored such that if you and your dog can complete the opening using just the lowest point obstacle and then get through obstacle seven within the established course time, you will qualify for any level.

The typical process for every agility run begins with each handler having access to a map (either a paper or electronic copy) that shows them where the red jumps are located and where the numbered obstacles, numbered two through seven, are positioned. When it's time for the event, the physical course is built by volunteers. Once the course is ready, the handlers have five to ten minutes (as set by the judge) to walk the course and strategize their opening sequence. This can be a stressful time, as each handler is determining the best course for their team, depending on their goals for the run.

During Snooker walkthroughs, I often overhear that a course feels too tight for large dogs or too long for small dogs. As the obstacles increase in points, they become more challenging to complete. If you cannot make it through obstacle seven within the set course time, you will need to strategize a higher point opening. As Heidi aged, I faced the added challenge that if the A-frame was obstacle number five or six, I had to come up with a higher point value in the opening to qualify, because we stopped doing the A-frame later in her career due to health and safety concerns for Heidi.

This game of Snooker is complex and challenging for beginners to understand. The opening is all about strategy. You can choose a simpler opening, keeping the dog close and doing basic maneuvers to get through to the closing. Another strategy some handlers employ is to complete a red jump and then the seven-point obstacle three times in the opening, which would give them a perfect score of fifty-one if they successfully navigate the closing sequence before the time is up. We call this the "go big or go home" strategy! I was never able to achieve this with

Heidi, but it is exciting to watch other teams attempt it. Most teams end up somewhere in the middle, choosing a course that they think flows well for their team and that they can complete cleanly.

When walking through the course after it is built (walk-throughs are only for handlers, not dogs), my invisible pretend dog always does precisely what I want it to do. After the walkthrough, I am confident we have a solid strategy to execute together. I've studied the course map and spent five to ten minutes during the walkthrough planning my plan. After we walk, I try to visualize the course that I created and reaffirm my goal for the upcoming run. If possible, it's also beneficial to observe other competitors to see their strategy unfold. However, you also should be cautious not to let their runs distract you from your plan. I can confirm firsthand that it's challenging to run a course you did not walk. And as a four-inch dog team, we were often first on the line when the run order was small to tall, and we were the guinea pigs for others to learn from.

In dog agility, as in life, all kinds of outside forces can impact your plan.

Now comes the execution of the plan, despite any distractions in the ring. In dog agility, these distractions could be ordinary things like:

- What dog ran before you?
- What dog is running after you?
- Did someone drop food in the ring?
- Is there an interesting smell in the corner?
- Is there a stranger on the course that your dog wants to meet?
- Does the judge look scary that day (i.e., for Heidi, men in hats)?

- Is there a great view from the top of the A-frame obstacle?

You get the idea. And we haven't even begun to talk about the course you came up with, and if your canine partner will agree that it's the best one.

Here is a typical scenario: You begin at the start line with your dog, and they jump over the first red jump obstacle. Success! Next, you head to the first numbered obstacle you selected, and you hit that exactly according to plan. You go to the second red jump and do your second numbered obstacle, and everything's going great. Awesome! Then, you reach the third red jump, and the dog knocks the bar, causing it to fall to the ground. Oh no! When a red jump bar goes down, the crowd groans collectively. We have all been there, and we know the challenge ahead for the team to maintain that run together. Therefore, you must pivot in real-time before the dog heads to the third-numbered obstacle. You hope for a clear path to that fourth red jump, wherever it may be on the course, and it's usually never where you are. You try to get that fourth red jump, pick up your last numbered obstacle, and cleanly reach obstacle two to complete your finishing sequence.

It's a fun game to watch because you never know what course each team will try in the opening and how they may try to recover if the plan goes sideways! And yes, this has happened to Heidi and me. We almost saved our run after a dropped red bar, reaching the fourth red jump, but Heidi decided to take a bonus obstacle on the way to jump number two. Our run was done, just like that. Sometimes, the plan fails during execution, despite the best evasive maneuvers and thorough preparation. And I almost forgot to mention that there is always a jump to stop the time at the end of Snooker. Wherever you are on the course, when the buzzer sounds or you hear a "Thank you" from the judge, you must go to that final jump to stop and lock in your time and points. You can have a blazing, perfect run, but it is non-qualifying (NQ) if you don't do the final jump. Again, I'm speaking from experience here, and it still hurts.

I may be in the minority, but I adore the game of Snooker. Ironically, that was one of the last championship agility titles that Heidi earned before she was paralyzed. I love the challenge of creating our own opening, understanding the points, and knowing how to earn the necessary score to qualify. I thoroughly enjoy watching the various strategies different teams try and cheering for the ones that go big and earn a perfect score of fifty-one.

Developing flexibility in a sport like dog agility can directly translate into improved work and life flexibility. Flexibility is about our capacity to modify our mindset and actions to solve problems. Sometimes, this needs to happen in the heat of the moment; alternatively, it can be a process that unfolds over time. There is a common project management philosophy to "Plan the plan, then execute!" This is an oversimplified statement for a complex process that can vary significantly depending on the circumstances. If only it were always that basic, and other things didn't get in our way once we began executing our fantastic plan! We also want to ensure that we are still following our plan, not someone else's, and resist getting pulled off course by other influences. Remember to figuratively "run the course you walked." Many factors can derail work and life plans, and some plans seem to go off course rapidly. It's even faster in dog sports. Plans can go off course in just seconds in agility, but we can learn from those experiences and apply them to other facets of our lives.

Learning to Pivot

Snooker is a perfect example of how being capable of pivoting in real-time and having incredible flexibility with your team can allow you to overcome a problem and succeed. It's a challenging game. You plan the plan, and perhaps your execution is flawless. But then a wrench is often thrown in, and you must pivot to find a new path to success. Luckily, real-life situations are not usually as fast as the split-second decisions we need to make in agility. So, how do we learn to be flexible, and what characteristics contribute to success in this regard?

One of the most significant variables I've found to impact flexibility is experience. More often than not, a new handler in agility cannot just adapt on the fly in a snooker opening. Experienced handlers frequently have the upper hand in such scenarios. In life, with age (and experience) comes wisdom. Employees with longer tenure, and older people in general, simply have more situational expertise to draw on when faced with a challenge. These experiences offer a broader perspective, which can result in greater flexibility when the plan goes sideways. Keep in mind, however, that experience isn't everything. Sometimes raw grit, determination, and a bold mindset can bring incredible flexibility, as beginners are not saddled with a "but we always do it this way" mentality that experience can bring.

Another key component of flexibility and problem-solving is planning. If you're playing Snooker, do you know where all four red jumps are? Or did you only check the three that you needed? If one of those drops out, simply knowing the location of the fourth one is a game-changer. It is critical to have a Plan B if things do not follow course or fall into place as planned. Sometimes, this alternative plan can be as common as a minor degree or certificate in college to fall back on if your major has limited career opportunities. It can mean knowing the locations of several parking garages near your interview in case the first one is full. It could also mean having an alternate speaker lined up for your event in case the primary speaker backs out. Advanced planning and preparation can give you the confidence to change course quickly, keeping your goals in focus. (This is such an important topic that I have dedicated an entire section to it in the Mentality chapter.)

What can happen to our flexibility when we have a weak link and our plans fall apart? In agility, your dog can instantly NQ your Snooker run in less than ten seconds, simply by going over two red jumps in succession when you didn't anticipate that path. Though your ego may be bruised, you brush it off and try again next time.

In your professional life, the collapse can be much slower and more extensive. Would you believe a renowned full-day speaker at a national conference had no backup plan for their full-day continuing education session? None of the online resources or links they had embedded in their presentation worked. They did not have a copy of the resource they referenced directly on the presentation laptop or flash drive. They did not have the resource pulled up as a separate tab that could be accessed outside of the presentation if the link didn't work. And somehow, the presenter had not verified whether they had access to a network before the presentation, so they could skip a link that didn't work. This utter lack of preparation left the presenter with zero flexibility. While it was memorable for all the wrong reasons, as an attendee at the conference, I absorbed many important lessons that went well beyond the day's stated learning objectives.

Experience inherently enables you to be more flexible. A way to make up for a lack of experience is to study and become a subject matter expert. Knowledge, expertise, and sheer determination will enable you to draw on the resources you need to make split-second decisions and pivot when the going gets tough. Preparation and planning are also keys to success. These things all help you be prepared for unexpected situations, which require you to pivot and change course quickly.

Recalculate

Change is hard! I recently attended a virtual learning session hosted by a wealth management group on retirement investing. They showed a slide that I found significant to people like me in Generation X. The slide showed four economic downturns: one that occurred during the early 1990s, the housing mortgage crisis of 2008, the COVID-19 pandemic in 2020, and then the recent declines in 2025. These downturns forced us all to pivot in some way, not only to survive but also to thrive in these challenging situations.

This slide caused me to reflect on my career. After graduating from college, I had a challenging time landing my first job. I'd attended a top design program at a prestigious university. Therefore, I would have multiple opportunities to choose from, right? Wrong! The tough economy in the early 1990s significantly impacted recent college graduates like me, as there was intense competition for a limited number of available jobs. Remember, we didn't have the Internet to research companies, email to reach out to potential employers, LinkedIn for referrals or connections, or job search engines like Indeed or Monster.com. When I graduated, there were few entry-level opportunities in my field despite my education and previous work experience. Most companies were simply not hiring due to the current economic conditions. I sent out well over a hundred cover letters and resumes to commercial interior design companies that I'd researched at the library, and none of those panned out.

After a six-month search, I landed my first industry job at a company owned by a family connection. Although it wasn't the job at a prominent architectural firm I had dreamed about, it was my only option, and I was highly grateful for the opportunity. Once I took the job, I realized one of the skills I had worked hard to develop would set me apart from everyone else in the office. That particular skill kept me employed for about six months longer than many other people during a round of layoffs common in my industry. Was it my favorite thing to do? No, but I realized that it was something I could do that others were not trained in, and it would allow me some flexibility in my career. And it continues to do so to this day! Consider additional training or certifications that you could earn to make yourself more invaluable to your team.

Nurture a special skill, interest, or expertise that you have, which could set you apart from your peers.

I am an accidental entrepreneur. Initially, I dreamed of being the head of a large design department at a prestigious architectural firm. But after many long hours and a lot of hard work early in my career, as I got closer to attaining that goal, I realized that it was no longer what I wanted. I achieved a certain level of success while working for others, but I often found the speed of reaction to opportunities and challenges to be cumbersome. So, I left and started my company, recognizing that I wanted to be more nimble than a large, often inflexible company. I had also studied ways to modify and improve project outcomes and client satisfaction.

Over the years, I have secured new opportunities by being open to different paths and having creative ideas to overcome obstacles. There is no inherent quick success in being adaptable, but there is sustained longevity, the more flexible your approach is overall.

Consider this in the same way that structural engineers approach building designs. The tallest buildings need to have some movement to withstand high winds. Stadiums require some movement in their structure to withstand crowds jumping up and down during an event. (At least that was what I kept telling myself during the Taylor Swift Eras Tour in Pittsburgh, as the stands literally bounced!). If these structures were inflexible, they would simply break. We can be guided by these principles to better value our talents and build flexibility into our plans and goals, ensuring we don't break under pressure.

In your work life, what preparations have you made that could give you more flexibility when things get tough? Lean into your special, unique talents, abilities, and interests, as those will set you apart from others. Even if you don't think you are adaptable, I believe that you are. Think about the entirety of the pandemic. Flexibility was key to adapting to that situation. Work that previously required in-person attendance became remote. Meetings that were always done in person became virtual. We had to devise new ways to accomplish tasks due to situations beyond our control. That time was marked both by roadblocks and by opportunities that continue to impact our lives today— and we are still adapting.

Innovation

Flexibility is not solely about our actions; it's also about our mindset. Modifying goals and adjusting aspirations can also lead to greater flexibility. As you go on your journey, one of your goals may be out of reach for some reason, so you need to adapt. You may have faced a setback for reasons outside your control or underestimated the effort required to achieve the accomplishment. Or you may realize that the way it's always been done is no longer the best way to do something, and things need to change.

Mindset is one of the keys to being flexible and achieving your goals. The competitors who step to the line when walking through Snooker and feel that the course is impossible or flat-out say, "I hate Snooker!" could often be the ones who struggle the most. They are giving up before they begin. What if instead of saying that you hate Snooker, you think, *Snooker is really challenging. What are some steps that I can take to find some success?"* What if instead of thinking that the course is impossible, you acknowledge that it may just be a challenging course and work to identify the traps that might impact you and your team?

The same goes for your work. What if, instead of saying, "I hate making cold calls!" you choose to be more flexible in your situation and find a way to reduce that need by generating more referrals? Instead of saying, "I hate doing presentations!" you consider working on the skills that will make you more effective and perhaps change your attitude about that activity?

If someone hates Snooker, they may never come to appreciate it. However, applying some of these tactics may help them reconsider that the situation may not be as bad as initially thought. With some effort, they can improve their flexibility and thereby achieve greater success. This will help them become more resilient and flexible overall.

View challenges as opportunities, and believe in your ability to handle whatever comes your way.

I often reflect on my long journey with Heidi in agility. We started in Teacup Agility, which is reduced equipment sizes, including smaller tunnels, narrower planks, smaller jumps, and shorter courses overall. This was all that we knew in the beginning. Our first teachers competed in Teacup Agility, and the training classes were conveniently located near our house. Though we struggled during our competitive time in Teacup, we did earn champion-level success (twice!). But there was a time when it became evident that Heidi was struggling with the requirements in that venue. The course times were becoming too tight (meaning our aging team was losing speed), and she was unable to earn qualifying runs for several reasons. But it was all that we knew.

However, I did not believe that Heidi was ready to retire. So, if Teacup Agility wasn't a good fit for us anymore, what other options did we have? I took a more flexible approach to explore what else might be available. We ventured into AKC Agility for a year and eventually transitioned to Canine Performance Events (CPE) Agility, where we competed for the remainder of her career. So, our team's flexibility came from acknowledging where we were competing, what we knew, and what we had trained for, which was no longer serving us. However, our skills and abilities could be transferred to something different.

Are you stuck in your career or a job you don't love? Are you being inflexible about how you branded yourself and what you're capable of with your skills and abilities? Perhaps if you have a more flexible approach, you can find a new venue for your success, just like Heidi and I did in CPE for many more years. This mindset shift has helped me home in on the things I'm good at and enjoy. It's also provided the flexibility to pivot to new opportunities when the time is right. The value of preparation, learning from failure, and having the confidence to pivot when situations change are some keys to adaptability.

Photo Credit: Virginia Weida

Winning Adaptability Strategies:
- **Think ahead.**
- **Reframe challenges.**
- **Have more than one plan.**
- **Redefine success when necessary.**

HEIDI'S PAWS FOR THOUGHT:

Keep people on their toes and take the path that's best for you.

Chapter Six - Teamwork

My teammate is different from me in almost every way. She is fierce; I am composed (mostly). She is shorter than average; I am tall. She is brunette; I am blond. She breaks the rules; I try to follow them. We don't even speak the same language! None of these sounds like the makings of a successful partnership. Yet, by developing trust and respect for each other, we are stronger partners because of our differences, and we love to win as a team.

Heidi was my first competition dog. Agility was the venue where we spent the most time competing. Heidi had naturally gifted abilities for it, and I loved that it was a physical and mental activity I could do with my dog (kind of like a timed 3-D strategy puzzle). Developing our teamwork in agility was a long and slow process. Heidi was a born leader, and it took a lot of convincing and work on my part for her to realize she could also have fun and win as a team with me!

In canine sports, teamwork exemplifies true partnership and takes considerable time to build. The relationship between a canine and its handler evolves depending on the sport. It has a push-and-pull dynamic that varies according to the situation and task at hand. There are activities where the handler leads more, and there are some where the canine leads more. However, regardless of the venue, you must rely on your partner to do their part. It requires earning trust from both partners, and that trust is built on a foundation of consistent behavior, mutual respect, competence, and follow-through.

Agility is a handler-led sport. Humans take the lead, as our skill set is more heavily utilized to guide us on a path to achieve the win. We understand the rules of the game and can follow last-minute instructions, as well as read numbered course maps. The human reviews the course, interprets it, and then walks it when set up (without the dog) to determine the best handling techniques. Then it is run as a team, with the dog hopefully completing all the obstacles according to the handler's instructions and guidance in the correct order and under the maximum course time. Although our partners may suggest that they can read the numbers one through twenty without help, we don't really believe they can do so without assistance. I could not compete in agility without my teammate, who is highly skilled at completing all the obstacles, and had to learn to follow my directions. It's more like a 60/40 share of the load, with the human having the greater share of the responsibility.

The canine must learn various core competencies to complete the obstacles safely and correctly, but there are also competencies for the human handler. Handlers must understand how their dogs will navigate the course and then be in the right place at the right time to provide them with direction. Handlers need to identify potential distractions that could divert the dogs off course, so they are prepared (sometimes referred to as "traps" by competitors). Handlers guide the dogs safely through contact obstacles, which require them to come up off the floor on narrow planks, often at top speed. To do all of these things, handlers work on tasks such as reading a dog's line (i.e., where the dog should be positioned while navigating obstacles) and utilizing common handling maneuvers, including front, rear, and blind crosses (i.e., ways for the handler to move to the opposite side of the dog).

It took lots of training for me to get up to speed (pun intended) to support Heidi, and I still train to this day. In videos of national and international competitions, the handlers make it look so easy! That belies years of training on their part, both individually and with their canine partner. To compete in agility as a team, both the handler and the canine must possess competence, follow-through, and consistent behaviors, trusting each other to do their part. Heidi was gifted athletically and needed to train to work as a team, while I had team leadership experience but needed to learn the agility skills.

In some other canine sports, such as Scent Work and Barn Hunt, my partner, Heidi, is the lead. The canine is in charge because they inherently possess the required skill set and hold the keys to the team's success. These sports rely on a canine's natural abilities, especially their incredible sense of smell. In Canine Scent Work, dogs are trained to alert on four specific scents that are hidden within a determined search area. In Barn Hunt, dogs are tasked with finding and discriminating between PVC tubes that contain a live rat and tubes that contain only bedding (no rats are harmed in this sport!). All the tubes are buried in a search area made of hay bales.

Canines possess a significantly greater number of olfactory receptors than humans, meaning they can smell roughly forty times better than we can. A common example is a bomb-sniffing dog at the airport. The human relies on the dog to indicate where there may be something suspicious, as the handler might not be able to detect the dangerous substances. Unlike in agility, the dog takes the lead in the course based on its sense of smell. I cannot smell where the rats or the scents are, and I can offer no help in the core premise of the sport. In such events, it is my responsibility to understand the overall rules and, most importantly, to interpret the dog's signals and communicate the information effectively to achieve a win. The canines absolutely have the most significant share of the load for winning in these sports.

In our successful partnership, which we worked hard to establish, Heidi and I took turns leading to achieve success. The more highly-qualified team member took the lead when the situation warranted it. This collaborative approach sustained our teamwork. Cross-training among different canine sports helped us build greater trust in our partnership, and our team was stronger because we acknowledged each other's strengths and learned from our weaknesses, as well as how we could better support one another. If we were not working together as a team, we could not possibly win.

Collaboration and teamwork are also essential components of success.

Although I have been a sole proprietor for over nineteen years, every project I work on in the commercial real estate industry involves a team of professionals, which can include owners, real estate professionals, architects, engineers, contractors, movers, furniture vendors, and others. My teams vary from project to project, but the foundation remains the same, based on what we learned in our earliest days in the industry. Each member has an important part to play and needs to rely on one another to accomplish the task.

I recently attended a conference where the keynote motivational speaker, Robyn Benincasa, an extreme adventure race competitor and world champion, described her adventures competing in the championships with her team and how critical each team member's skills were to their success. In these competitions, teams of four athletes, which are required to include both male and female members, race through remote regions of the world, participating in trail running, biking, canoeing, climbing, and repelling over several days. There are rules about how they must stay together and that all members must complete all sections of the course.

What she described in her session was an extreme example of how team members' strengths can support one another's weaknesses, highlighting the importance of trading off leadership roles and setting aside egos, with memorable examples demonstrating that trust is the key to winning. To see further examples of this, I would also recommend watching the movie *Arthur the King*, inspired by another adventurer, Mikael Lindnord, who not only became close with his teammates but also forged a bond with a dog while racing through the Dominican Republic. It shows you a (Hollywood) version of a team being pushed to their limits, leaning on each other's strengths, while maintaining loyalty—all with a dog! (I would caution you about watching it while on an airplane, though, because I could barely hold it together during parts of the drama.) Our teamwork examples will rarely be this extreme in real life, but these are great concepts to build on.

Partnership

A common motivational saying is that there is "no I in team," implying that collaboration is more important than ego. By definition, teams are comprised of more than one entity, and they win and lose together. A partnership can involve more than two parties, but the approach remains the same, regardless of the number of partners. And there's no doubt in my mind that competing in any dog sport builds skills that can be applied to any team situation in life. In canine sports, it's most often a team of two, and you become close partners because it requires one of the highest levels of teamwork. Sports partnerships frequently feature incredible athletes who excel together, such as some of the outstanding ice dancing teams and volleyball duos. There are also countless examples of successful business partnerships, including those between business partners, sibling partners, and spouses who may be partners both in life and in business.

The process of developing teamwork with your dog is more intense than most human partnerships, except for our life partners. Establishing a partnership with an animal is a skill that requires considerable effort and dedication. At the outset, you must establish a level of trust, which can take time, depending on the situation. You spend twenty-four hours a day, seven days a week, together with your dog. They are entirely dependent on you for all needs. There is a language barrier, and you have to work hard to communicate with a being that is unlike you in every way. In fact, beyond basic life needs of eating, drinking, breathing, and sleeping, you have little in common. These are just a few of the teamwork barriers we face immediately when training an animal.

Some of us also face a significant size difference with our partners. Speaking from experience, an almost six-foot human training an eight-inch dog comes with many unique challenges, just as training a larger dog could be for a smaller person. We are outside the norm on both ends: I am in the top percentile of height for humans, and my canine partner is in the bottom percentile of height for canine sports. This height difference has presented challenging situations to overcome during training. Consider the difference in training a German Shepherd, whose mouth is roughly at your waist, versus a dachshund, whose mouth is near your ankles. Our communication patterns are different and adjusted due to the differences in our height.

If each of us were asked to visualize what a partnership looks like, I suspect most people would come up with a graphic of equal parts. Two team members would be represented identically, indicating an equal share of the workload. However, in reality, a business partnership, for example, can have two or more partners with varying ownership percentages, depending on the type of business structure that is formed. And the strongest teams may not necessarily be those that are equal in ability. They are more like a yin-yang relationship where the strengths of one team member support the weaknesses of the other.

A phrase we often hear a lot in training is "trust your dog." Just like with any other relationship, it usually works out to trust them, but sometimes they let us down. Some courses demand complete trust in your canine partner to win; often, they do what is required, but sometimes they can't. There are other times when a dog seemingly ignores the handler's request to do something on a course, and it turns out that the dog was correct and the team qualifies (despite the human)! It's unusual, but it does happen, and we usually get a good laugh out of it. To be honest, when there is a mistake that causes a non-qualifying run or score, it is more often than not the fault of the human part of the team. It can be a humbling experience.

All of the work I have done with Heidi to establish a partnership with a star player like her has positively impacted teamwork in other facets of my life. Success in agility is not possible if the dog leads, just as success in Scent Work is not possible if the human takes the lead. I have witnessed this many times in my career. Recognizing the innate abilities of team members, working toward common goals, and respecting one another will build trust within any partnership. The team will be more successful when all of the members collaborate rather than compete, supporting the member who has the best abilities for the task at hand to take the lead.

Communication

Effective and clear communication is crucial to completing any work or project successfully. Communication can take many forms: written, verbal, and nonverbal, with body language playing a significant role in how others perceive us. Dogs, like people, generally respond well to verbal cues, while some dogs can work with mostly nonverbal cues. In some circumstances, you may only be able to use one type of communication or another. For example, I have friends with deaf dogs, and all of their communication is nonverbal. I also know teams where a handler may not be able to keep up with their dog, so they train the dog more on verbal cues, which allows them to perform the course with the handler more or less in the center of the ring. Both of these extremes are a joy to watch perform. It is incredible what can be overcome by adapting communication styles.

Examples of verbal cues for dogs given by their handlers are familiar to most. These can include commands like "sit," "stay," and "down." Early on in basic dog training, I realized that combining the sit, stay, and down verbal commands with a nonverbal cue or gesture can help your dog learn the commands more quickly and be more reliable. In fact, there are often handling tricks that require a series of only nonverbal cues to be given to your dog, and your dog needs to comply. Handlers start with training both verbal and nonverbal cues together and reward the desired behavior. Then they slowly fade the verbal command until the dog does the trick with just the nonverbal sign. It's certainly fun to watch the connection established between those canines and their handlers.

In the sport of agility, we begin by teaching the dog a combination of verbal and nonverbal cues for the equipment and skills we teach them. Using both verbal and nonverbal cues together can be challenging for handlers to master as we learn all of the new commands, along with where we need to be physically on the course. Nonverbal cues in agility are all about the body: where the handler's eyes are looking, where the shoulders and chest are pointing, which direction the feet are moving, and whether an arm is raised or lowered. All of these things are forms of non-verbal communication with the dog, and any of them can impact your overall success in a run.

As you begin to enter competitions, it can be challenging in this fast-paced sport to learn to use both verbal and non-verbal communication effectively. I am guilty of using the wrong verbal command while physically showing the correct obstacle. It also confounds me how many obstacles in agility start with the letter T, such as teeter, tunnel, and tire. They are so easy for me to mix up! When I'm in a one-minute sprint or less, managing where I am and where my dog is, I'm often unable to call out the right verbal cues, so I tend to rely more on nonverbal ones. Luckily, the dogs adapt to their humans and follow the most obvious cue (usually a physical cue over a verbal one for my team). For example, if I show the A-frame and say "tunnel," Heidi will typically take the A-frame. There is a time and a place for both styles of communication, and I am continually working to improve my use of verbal cues.

Communication is a two-way street, so we also need to consider how our dogs are communicating with us. Dogs also communicate verbally and nonverbally. They bark, whine, cry, and make a variety of verbal noises. The most obvious nonverbal communication example is a wagging tail. But as you spend more time with dogs, you realize that they have different speeds or ways that they may wag their tail, which can have completely different meanings. To understand the dog's communication, you also need to consider the position of its ears, eyes, facial expressions, and overall body language, as well as its tail. When you closely train with your animal, you can learn to recognize when they are happy, stressed, hurt, or sometimes just hungry by observing their behavior and nonverbal communication. And when you cross-train in canine-led sports such as Scent Work, the handler needs to focus on the nonverbal cues from the animal to know when they are trying to tell them that they have found something. It is essential to be in tune with your canine partner and what they may be trying to communicate to you both verbally and non-verbally. Learning to pay attention to your canine partner in turn helps you communicate better with humans.

I learned from my daughter's teachers that students are a combination of visual (nonverbal) and auditory (verbal) learners, and some students prefer one learning style over the other. This provides a greater understanding as I work with others. As leaders, we need to recognize that some team members may require written instructions, while others may follow verbal instructions more effectively. We may feel that newer team members are simply unable to follow instructions, but perhaps we are not communicating them effectively. It can be frustrating for us as leaders to have to use a different style of communication than the one we prefer, but we need to have patience and learn the most effective method for our team. Just like with canine teams, there are extremes, but most of us work best with a combination of verbal and nonverbal cues.

Awareness of communication styles is essential for building a team's success.

One of my favorite sessions while teaching business practices to interior design students was presenting on business etiquette and personal power. In addition to reviewing networking and interview tips, we talked about the importance of strong communication and body language. We discussed how seventy to ninety percent of human communication is conveyed through nonverbal cues, which include factors such as clothing, body language, posture, gestures, and facial expressions. It is essential to present the "total package" when making a first impression, such as at a job interview or sales presentation. This includes proper attire, grooming, and body language, along with effective verbal communication. This also holds when working with clients and leading teams.

Though we don't have the wagging tail, our nonverbal communications are pretty similar to canines. When you see someone with slumped shoulders, always looking down, and fidgeting with their hands, you could make assumptions that they are not interested. The best resume and qualifications won't get you the job if you have poor posture and a weak handshake and never make eye contact. Suppose you are rallying your team to work on a significant, deadline-driven project. In that case, the tone of your voice, combined with facial expressions and body language, is key in motivating your team.

Active listening when others are speaking, along with general awareness of your team members, helps with both human and canine teams. If I had started an agility run with Heidi and not made eye contact, used an off-tone (i.e., too soft or too harsh), and shuffled my feet, we may never have achieved a qualifying score. Working with dogs has made me a much better communicator overall, with a greater awareness of the significance that nonverbal communication plays.

Leadership

Leaders cannot be successful on their own. Success almost always requires collaboration and a group effort, with top teams possessing diverse skill sets. The road to management can be a rocky one, and it can be frustrating to be tasked to lead a project and a team when the members are dissimilar and inexperienced. You quickly realize you have nothing in common and may believe you are set up to fail. This has happened to me, as the commercial real estate industry needs a team of people for almost every project.

In a previous role, I observed that our company experienced high turnover, particularly in entry-level positions. Architecture is a challenging industry, characterized by long hours and heavy workloads, which can make it difficult to find one's place. Employers make a concerted effort to foster diversity in the office to find new hires. When professionals from different countries come to America, however, their qualifications do not always translate to the same level of position in the United States that they may have earned. This is similar to physicians and other skilled occupations: each country has its specific requirements, so retraining may be needed to meet these particular requirements. As a result, highly qualified professionals may have to take entry-level positions.

As a mid-sized company, much of the office was involved in multi-year, large-scale projects, while my core clientele projects were smaller with a faster turnaround. I often found myself mentoring new hires on my teams, as they were easier to add to shorter-term projects. Many of them spoke multiple languages, and the diversity made us stronger all around. Patience and listening skills were the keys to leading our team to success on our projects. The best leaders offer trust and support to their team, establish clear goals and roles, communicate effectively, collaborate, value diverse perspectives, and continually seek ways to enhance their performance. I recognized the necessity of these qualities and had been honing them through years of experience with my dogs.

Developing and training a team follows a similar process each time. Once you have created one team, you may become complacent, assuming it is always a similar process. However, there can be significant variability depending on the team members. Just ask a dog trainer if training all dogs is the same. They will agree that the general process is the same, but the variability in success lies in the fact that each dog is different. Even dogs of the same breed, their siblings, or their offspring will be different from each other. I developed my partnership with Heidi and have been able to apply that process to my other dogs, but each one that has followed has had specific needs from me that vary from one another. This is similar to our personal lives, where the people closest to us have varying needs and expectations.

In our global economy, with digital work tools, it is not out of the question that you may face teamwork challenges at work due to variations in time zones, languages, and overall working styles. Working with training dogs and establishing our partnerships to compete has taught me to have greater patience with others at work and in life. After the flexibility, dedication, and patience required to form a partnership with Heidi, I believe it is possible to find and nurture common ground with anyone.

Patience is a quiet yet essential leadership skill.

Teamwork is central to developing leadership skills. Canine sports teams exemplify some of the best characteristics of successful team leadership: trust, shared common goals, compassion for fellow team members, and a compatible work ethic. These are all elements I've learned firsthand from my partnership with Heidi, and they can impact our personal and professional lives by either helping or hindering our drive for success.

Photo Credit: Life's Memories Photos by Lisa Urbassik

Winning Teamwork Strategies:

- **Communicate clearly.**
- **Build trust.**
- **Lead when you are strongest; follow when you are not.**
- **Embrace diversity.**

HEIDI'S PAWS FOR THOUGHT:

Do what your teammate means, not what they say.

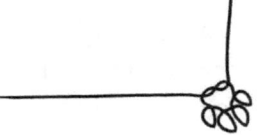

Chapter Seven - Reward

Heidi and I entered a special Friday evening CPE trial locally. They were playing a game that we needed for our championship title, and I thought it would be fun to come out and earn another qualifying run to get us closer to our goal. So, I finished up work early, and we headed out. It was a reasonable course for our abilities, and I felt pretty confident. The run order that evening was tall-to-small, so I watched the other teams and awaited our turn. Being a four-inch jump height team, we were close to (if not) last in the run order.

Most dogs were doing well on the course and earning their Qs. After more than seventy dog-and-handler teams, it was finally our turn. So, we stepped to the line, and off we went. Or rather, off I went. The opening was simple: a bar jump, then a tunnel that curved to the right. I had started Heidi on my left, and she went right over the jump to start the time. Then, rather than enter the tunnel, she veered sharply to the left and ran about five more feet behind it. To my astonishment, she stopped on a dime and plopped her butt down to sit and munch on a dog treat she had found on the course. The treat was so big that she actually had to sit down to eat it all.

I was stunned. First of all, no handler is allowed to bring treats into the competition ring—

not in their hands, pockets, or anywhere else. In fact, food or treat holders are not allowed within ten feet of the ring. So, how did the treat get there? Secondly, how did seventy-plus dogs run this course ahead of us and all miss that cookie in that ring? It was a little out of the way of the dogs' path, but I still could not believe that Heidi found it or even knew it was there. She must have known as soon as we entered the ring. After she licked her lips, she finally went through the tunnel for me.

After that, the rest of the run went precisely as you would imagine: slow as molasses. Heidi had her nose to the ground, sniffing hopefully for another treat. Because, surely, this must be the magical place where cookies fall from the sky! We were so far over time, it was ridiculous. But how could I be mad at her? In her defense, if you were at the gym and found a crumpled twenty-dollar bill when no one else was around, I bet you would spend a minute or two looking for more, am I right? We will never know where that cookie came from, but in that moment, an unintended reward actually pulled us off track from accomplishing the goal. Rewards are vital, both for humans and dogs, but the right timing is critical as well.

Animal training is extraordinarily reward-based. Whether or not you have any pets at home, you have undoubtedly seen a show with trained animals doing incredible tricks. What do their handlers and trainers all have in common? They use a treat pouch or bucket to reward the animals when they exhibit the behavior they are trained to do. When you first get a new dog, whether it's a puppy or an older rescue, you begin teaching simple behaviors like "sit" or "down," and you reward them with a treat, such as a dog cookie. If they go to the bathroom outside, you reward their behavior by giving them a cookie. As your dog progresses in learning tricks or a sport, you ask for specific behaviors and reward them.

In agility, we start by training dogs to do basic jumps while keeping the bars up. We also need to train them to perform jumps in succession, which involves completing one jump and then driving to the next jump in line. We then expand from the different styles of jumps to the tunnel, which can be a challenge for some dogs. As the tunnels become longer and more curved, dogs cannot see the end when they enter at the beginning. We also have to train them for the contact obstacles, named so because they all have a painted yellow "contact zone" that the dog must put a paw in when passing through. These include an A-frame, a dogwalk, and the teeter or seesaw, which is often one of the hardest contacts to train because it moves under their body as they go across it. Last but not least is learning the weave poles, which is also a challenging behavior for many dogs. Teaching all of these new behaviors requires rewards of some kind, because dogs would never work on these skills without a reward system.

Celebrating significant milestones and small accomplishments alike is essential, even as adults.

Similar to animal training, we grow up with a reward system and mostly abandon it when we become adults. What were some of your favorite rewards growing up? Most of the rewards that I can remember from my childhood involved food. I learned things like how to dive headfirst into a pool and how to type on a real typewriter (yes, I am that old) for a McDonald's cheeseburger. When we performed well at school or had a band concert, we got to go out for ice cream. The trip home from vacation almost always included an ice cream stop to soften the blow of the long travel day and the return to work and school. Those were some of our family reward systems. In both our personal and work lives, setting and following a reward system can be crucial to avoiding burnout.

Compensation

Everybody wants to get paid fairly for doing work; nobody wants to work for free (including dogs). When we agree to take a job, we earn a salary that has been negotiated. If we achieve extraordinary results or the organization outperforms expectations, we may get bonuses. We, just like our dog, love special bonus awards. However, as these bonuses become commonplace or annual, you begin to expect them, and a change in either direction quickly catches your attention. We may not even be aware of this or have given it a second thought because it is so ingrained. But you can learn a great deal about a payment system by working with dogs, as they have absolute boundaries.

During the COVID-19 pandemic, we were doing some online tricks and exercises to keep the pups busy and engaged. It was a challenging time for our dogs as well, since they were accustomed to going on weekend adventures. Because basically everything was canceled, we had to look for new ways to enrich them.

One of the viral online challenges among dog owners at the time was to see how many puppy sit-ups your dog could do in a minute. One version of a puppy sit-up involves putting your dog in a sit position, then having them go to a down position, back up to a sit, and then finally to a down again. If you treated each one after completion, it would slow you down and reduce the total number completed in time. I was curious to see how many puppy sit-ups Heidi would do before she got a cookie. So, I set up my phone to record and started having her work. Heidi completed fifteen puppy sit-ups in twenty seconds, but then she absolutely refused to keep working until she got paid. She's always been one to make sure that she is compensated for her efforts!

I use the term "cookie," but dog rewards can be all manner of things, including both food and toys, and they can have varying values. Before I began our journey in agility, I mistakenly believed that all dog treats were equal and that they varied in value based mainly on cost. That is entirely false! There are both low-value dog treats, which in our world are Cheerios, as well as high-value treats, such as Braunschweiger (liver sausage) squares or meatballs, which we referred to as "puppy crack." Some dogs value toys more than treats as rewards. The bottom line is that each dog is different, and it just takes a little trial and error to find out what motivates them most.

So, how do you effectively use low-value and high-value treats? For routine behaviors, low-value treats are fine. It keeps their arousal at a manageable level, and they get compensated fairly for their work. When you are training something new or working through a more challenging behavior, however, you'll want to use a higher-value treat, which can affect arousal noticeably. For example, Heidi would run so much faster in class as soon as the meatballs came out. Keep in mind, if you use high-value treats excessively, the reward value diminishes. The true purpose of using high-value treats is to reinforce the desired behavior, keeping the dog interested while acknowledging that the behavior was a challenge.

Another essential reward concept is known as the "jackpot." This reward is most often used when a trainer is working on a particular behavior, and the dog is struggling. When the dog finally learns the behavior, it's treated to a reward jackpot—a rapid stream of cookies (like a slot machine spitting out coins). This not only raises their arousal, but it also shows dogs that you really liked what they did. This can also be done with a high-value toy by having extra play time together.

For employees of a company, there are often reward systems beyond salary that are embedded in the work culture. If you put in so many years, you may earn a new status. If you work hard, you may be eligible for a new title that comes with higher pay. These reward systems can be complicated to figure out when it's unclear how many accomplishments or successes are required before you become promoted and earn a raise. Sometimes you feel you deserve a bonus, but the company doesn't give you one. Inconsistent reward systems can sometimes make you work harder, but they can backfire as well if employees become frustrated.

Are you working for an organization where the rewards just aren't there? Are you getting low-value Cheerios when what you really want is a meatball? Assess your situation honestly and consider what your low-to-high reward value system might be. Think about the things that motivate you most. For humans, as opposed to dogs, it's a little more complicated because rewards don't necessarily have to be food-oriented. Sure, it can be that expensive ice cream treat—you know, the ones that are dark-chocolate-covered caramel and fantastic ice cream inside, which are probably a thousand calories but are so delicious! However, it could also be something tangible or even an experience. One way to reward yourself is to take a fifteen-minute walk outside to get some fresh air after completing tasks on your to-do list. Or maybe it's taking time to go to lunch with an old friend to reconnect. Perhaps it's an experience on your bucket list that you need to schedule or take that trip to a place you've only dreamed about. Another reward could be working summer hours, which would allow you to spend more time with your family and friends when the weather is nice.

Everyone's reward system will be unique.

And if you are an entrepreneur, it's still essential to have a system of rewards built in to celebrate your achievements. These rewards don't have to be grand. Do I sometimes stop for an ice cream treat on the way home after a long day? Do I sometimes treat myself to that special outfit or accessory that I've had my eye on after I achieve something new or in advance of an important meeting? Yes. Yes, I do. Do I take vacation days and time off to recover from working long hours or meeting project deadlines? (If I am being honest, that is still a work in progress. But those of you who own your own business know precisely what I'm talking about.) The bottom line is that it's undeniable that rewards work in driving success, just as they do for dogs. So, are you rewarding your efforts as you work, live, and play, or are you waiting for someone else to do it?

Recognition

In agility, each venue has established a clear and straightforward path for earning recognition and titles. In our early days of competing in agility, Heidi and I struggled to earn enough qualifying runs for our first title. Although most only required three, competing necessitates multiple trial entries (or more), especially when things go wrong. The frequency of the trials can also affect your success. Heidi and I sometimes had to wait six months between trials because they were only held twice a year in our area. Earning a championship in Teacup Agility seemed like an unattainable goal due to the significant number of required qualifying runs (forty-two, to be exact!). That said, we loved the activity, so we persevered.

As Heidi and I improved, we gradually began to accumulate qualifying runs and even earn a few titles. I began to realize that, with diligence, we really could achieve significant goals together and gain recognition for our achievements. We just needed to keep putting in the work, following the path that was laid out step by step, and trust in the process.

This is easier said than done, however, when the path is unclear. In our professional lives, the steps to achieve a new title at work (i.e., partner, senior manager, vice president, shareholder, etc.) may not be so obvious. As a result, you may need to pave your own path.

Some people crave recognition; others shy away from the spotlight. Throughout my career, I have heard repeatedly how women don't always feel comfortable discussing their accomplishments. Somehow, it became ingrained in our society that discussing one's accomplishments was taboo and seen as bragging or showing off. But if you're not sharing your achievements with others, how will anyone know? If you are waiting for someone to notice you and say, "Hey, good job," you may be waiting for a very long time. When you work for a large organization, recognition and rewards can seem few and far between. And if you are working for yourself, who will give you the recognition?

Self-advocacy goes hand in hand with rewards and recognition.

Self-advocacy is standing up for yourself with confidence, believing in your worth, and questioning authority when necessary. It is essential to be clear about what you are asking for (i.e., recognition, compensation, promotion), to set boundaries, and to occasionally accept outcomes that may not be in your favor.

Advocacy is one of my core values. Throughout my life and career, I have consistently felt like the underdog, which is why I always advocate for change, recognition, or opportunity. Over the years, for various reasons, I have gained extensive experience in self-advocacy through my involvement in canine sports. Sometimes it was verifying scores and recording qualified runs in a database. Other times, it was requesting an appeal from a judge on the day of the show. Advocating for yourself can be challenging work, but each time you do, you increase your power.

Some tips for success in practicing self-advocacy:

- Be assertive, not aggressive. Speak from your perspective, focusing on "I" statements.
- Stay calm and respectful. Remain composed whenever possible.

- Gather your facts, rehearse your pitch, and anticipate objections.
- Choose the right moment, and know your audience.
- Acknowledge other perspectives and prioritize what needs to be escalated.

Trust me, the more you do it, the easier it gets. And if you aren't doing this for yourself, who will?

If you are not receiving the recognition you desire within your workplace, consider applying for awards from professional associations. As Heidi and I achieved some success in agility, I became inspired to seek out some professional recognition for my career. So, utilizing the SMART goal-setting concept, I outlined specific steps for achieving skills and gaining experience, which would hopefully lead to greater recognition.

When applying for professional awards, be aware that even if you meet the published list of requirements, you may not necessarily earn that recognition right away. If you don't gain the recognition the first time around, consider applying the following year. This is persistence. This is perseverance. And I can tell you from personal experience that it has worked out for me and others as well. It feels good to achieve our goals and be recognized, and each time you're recognized, it brings you more confidence and success.

I also encourage other professionals in my network to seek recognition. When I see an award opportunity, for example, I try to think of anyone I know who might be a candidate. Nothing brings me greater joy than seeing the people in my network earn a well-deserved recognition. And once you gain that recognition, make sure to shout it from the rooftops!

Most people enjoy being acknowledged for their efforts, whether it's a grand gesture or just a simple one. This is a crucial consideration for all leaders, regardless of their level. Recognition at work and in the community can be as simple as a thank you from an organizer or a job well done from your boss. It could be formalized through a written accolade, sent via a group email, or posted on social media. It can also be a significant award in your area of expertise (i.e., teacher of the year, community member star award, first-place team at a national competition, etc.). Make sure you consider rewards not only for yourself, but also for those around you!

Return On Investment

Many people assume that when they hear the word "reward," it implies dollars. You may or may not be surprised to learn that there are very few financial awards in the sport of dog agility. It's quite the opposite. Why even do it, then? Think about it: there are lots of hobbies that demand a similar level of passion and a significant amount of time to both train and play the game, and many of these require money just to participate (golf comes to mind)!

The return on investment (ROI) for canine sports is that, first and foremost, you establish an incredible relationship with your animal. You and your dog learn and grow together in so many ways. The other significant ROI for me is the community that you gain when you are part of an activity like dog sports. You meet people from all different backgrounds, and you spend many hours with them. We support each other. We cheer for the highs and comfort each other through the lows, and we would do anything to help each other out if needed. Sure, the ribbons, medals, and awards are excellent reminders of our journey, and sometimes they are sentimentally precious beyond the cost of the materials to make them. But the thing that's the most rewarding for me is the community of connections that I have made through competing in agility.

And the community loves to celebrate your achievements as well, from your first title through to your championship. There is a whole tradition that when you earn your championship, you bring a human treat (most often a sheet cake), a treat for the dogs, and your championship bar (a PVC pipe with stickers added) for other competitors to sign. I can't think of any other competitive environment where the community does so much to celebrate each other's achievements, and it has changed my perspective to make sure I am equally celebrating others more in my life.

I have a similar approach to my return on investment for my professional career. I certainly want to be compensated for the work I do, but I also pride myself on ensuring the job is done to the best of my ability. Sometimes that means putting in more work than I anticipated to get it done correctly. A paycheck is important, but that is only part of the equation. Life is a balance, and in addition to compensation and reward, our return on investment is seeking a higher purpose, whether acknowledged or not! That means that I also volunteer some of my time to further causes that are fulfilling to me, such as championing women in commercial real estate, supporting other small businesses, and advocating for the interior design profession.

Personal fulfillment is so individual, and it is as unique as your goals. In a way, it's looking to answer the question of what your *why* is. My origin story of dog agility truly began after I adopted Heidi. I wanted to ensure that I took her to training classes, as it had been about fifteen years since I had had a puppy. Our agility journey became like a snowball rolling down a hill. It started small and picked up speed and size as it rolled. After our first puppy class, we tried other training classes to develop basic skills and then began our agility course training. From there, we were encouraged to attend a trial to see what it was all about, as they were seeking volunteers. So, I spent the afternoon at our training club and realized how much fun everyone was having with their dogs. If others could do it, I figured we could, too.

Six months later, I signed up to compete in the next trial. This led to more training and classes, which in turn led to more competitions, and ultimately resulted in success and more competitions. Now, here we are twelve years later, with over a hundred titles earned together as a team! Once I started down that path with Heidi, I also trained my subsequent rescue, Penny, in a similar manner. Though a completely different dachshund temperament than Heidi's, Penny also competed in agility and transferred over to Scent Work as she got older. She was an absolute star! I also had some success (and tons of fun) training my thirteen-year-old, Le Beau (adopted when he was twelve), in Scent Work. Which brings me to my current partner, Gus Gus, who has earned championship titles at the youngest age of any of my dogs. I've been able to apply the skills I learned with Heidi and other older dogs to my training and experiences with my youngest, and so far, it has been an incredible journey.

This experience correlates very strongly with professional experience. As you learn and work on different projects and gain expertise, you can do things more quickly and better, and build on that throughout your career.

Strive for fulfillment over success in everything you do.

I may have been considered "extra" when I was younger because I am energetic and tend to jump into things completely with both feet. I have high expectations for myself, and I have a strong work ethic to try to meet them. Now that I am well beyond the halfway point in my career, I strive for higher success at work, garner greater recognition, and maintain a balanced lifestyle, all the while fostering meaningful connections in everything I do. I feel that bringing these pieces together lends a greater authenticity to everything in my life. I believe that by considering the things you excel at outside of your career, you may find similar ways to apply them to other areas of your life and achieve more than you ever dreamed of. All work and no play would never work for Fluffy, and it shouldn't work for you, either!

Photo Credit: Virginia Weida

Winning Reward Strategies:
- **Recognize and celebrate achievements.**
- **Reward with purpose and timing.**
- **Advocate for yourself.**
- **Pursue personal fulfillment.**

HEIDI'S PAWS FOR THOUGHT:

Don't work for free.

Closing

When I think back on what would become our final days competing in agility, two memories in particular stand out, and they are life lessons that I still lean on today.

As we neared our improbable goal of a second CPE Championship Title, I began to feel the pressure to be perfect and earn every qualifying run possible. I knew the clock was ticking on our team's agility career, but I just didn't anticipate such a sudden end. As we closed in on the final ten qualifying runs we needed, I was already planning to drop Heidi back down to Level 1 courses so she could just do a few runs per trial, stay active and limber, and do what she loved. We just needed to get a couple more difficult (for us) runs out of the way, then it would be smooth sailing (famous last words).

When you are on the course with your dog, and you are stressed and really want to earn the qualifying score, it's interesting what all goes through your brain (at least my brain, anyway!). As I work hard to run fast and remember course numbers, all while handling my dog, I often lose the ability to verbalize first. My brain is hyper-focused on the physical aspects during those forty-five to sixty seconds, so my speech is limited, but I can still hear and process information.

In one of our last courses together, there was a big line of jumps at the finish that curved midway in the course, then ran right along the front ring gating. I was worried when I walked the course and saw how it finished, because there is so much distraction at the front course gating—dogs that just finished running, dogs waiting their turn to run, lots of noises and smells, and lots of people! Running to the gating was a favorite move for Heidi. She loved to sniff all the smells and go into hunting-hound mode to assess the "danger" on the other side of the gate to "protect" us. We would never make course time if she went over to the gating.

So, in my crazy handling style we had developed to win over the years, I found a way to take the much longer handler path to get to the outside of the course to keep Heidi from the gating. I vividly remember hearing someone say, "Why on earth is she taking the outside?" Then someone else replied, "Oh, she always does this with this dog to keep her dog going." Then the first person responded a second later with, "Oh wow, I didn't know dachshunds could run that fast!"

Run the course that is best for you.

The second memory comes from our last agility trial together in April of 2023. I needed one more qualifying run in a game that was so challenging for us, called Fullhouse. It is the handler's (or dog's) choice course, with no specified path to run set by the judge. The teams need to accumulate a high number of points, along with a "full house" of three one-point jumps, two three-point tunnels, and one five-point contact. I was nervous for my run and was stuck between two course routes I had come up with. I was pacing off the two options to see which was a shorter distance and considering my options (all within our five-minute course walk time). Competitors often share their course strategies with others, and as I was explaining my options, my friend looked me in the eye and said, "Just run, Virginia. Just run."

Just Run.

Her words were simple yet filled with deeper meaning—words she knew I needed to hear in that moment. With those words in my mind, we just ran, and we qualified, earning our last "hard" event. We were well on our way to finishing the championship title when, just a few days later, Heidi's discs blew and she had career-ending back surgery. Our agility time had come to a close.

I share these two stories because they were lessons about more than agility. Each person's journey to success is different. Even if you attend the same university, are in the same profession, or work for the same company, you cannot compare your success to the person beside you. You need to establish your keys to success and blaze the trail to accomplish those goals. Others may question your route, but don't let them deter you. Take the outside if you have to, even if it's the more challenging way. And don't get so hung up on second-guessing yourself that you stop making forward progress. Just run.

At fourteen and a half, with IVDD and Cushing's Disease, Heidi is still beating the odds. I appreciate the time I have left with her and enjoy her occasional zoomies in the yard with Gus Gus, as well as her snuggles in the evenings. I will forever be grateful for all the gifts that she has given me, many of which I have shared in this book. May we all use these gifts to go from underdogs to winning bitches.

If Heidi and I can do it, so can you.

Titles Earned in Heidi's Career:
CS-ATCH TACH2 Heidi RN NAP NJP NFP ACT2 TKA TMAG5 SpChCL
SpChSN C-SWE ETD CCF1 NSD TC1 GCHAS Peter CHPRCL CHPRSL
PLTCSL CHPLSB CHPRU PLTRULSB CCSS-L1 RATI THR1 FCR1

Photo Credit: Virginia Weida

From Underdog to Winning Bitch: How My Dachshund Inspired Me to Overcome Obstacles and Succeed Playbook

Winning Motivation Strategies:
- Embrace your authentic self.
- Lean into your passions.
- Persevere through adversity.
- Seek community and connection.

Winning Goals Strategies:
- Set SMART goals (Specific, Measurable, Achievable, Relevant, Time-Based).
- List actionable items.
- Plan ahead, measure progress, and adapt.
- Enjoy the journey, not just the outcome.

Winning Mentality Strategies:
- Take the first step.
- Embrace optimism without evidence.
- Never lose.
- Be outrageously confident.

Winning Training Strategies:
- Honestly assess shortfalls.
- Build strong foundations.
- Seek feedback and mentorship.
- Embrace lifelong learning.

Winning Adaptability Strategies:
- Think ahead.
- Reframe challenges.
- Have more than one plan.
- Redefine success when necessary.

Winning Teamwork Strategies:
- Communicate clearly.
- Build trust.
- Lead when you are strongest; follow when you are not.

- Embrace diversity.

Winning Reward Strategies:

- Recognize and celebrate achievements.
- Reward with purpose and timing.
- Advocate for yourself.
- Pursue personal fulfillment.

Personal Assessment Tool

Scan the QR Code for a link to a free self-assessment tool for these winning skills and traits:

Thank you

I hope you enjoyed these stories about Heidi and her incredible nuggets of wisdom for success that we can all learn from! Please consider leaving a review on Amazon or Goodreads, as well as sharing this book with your networks. I would really appreciate it!

I am available for speaking engagements and book signings at your future events. Please visit www.virginiaweida designs.com for more information on available sessions and topics.

You can also find me on Instagram and LinkedIn for professional postings, and on Facebook for all things dog sports!

Cheers to finding your own path to success!

<u>Heidi's PAWS for Thought</u>

Follow your heart's desires.

Never underestimate what you are capable of.

Practice is overrated. Be confident.

Showcase your innate ability.

Keep people on their toes and take the path that's best for you.

Do what your teammate means, not what they say.

Don't work for free.

Glossary

Here is a quick glossary of agility terms to help readers follow along. These descriptions are all in my words, not technical definitions. For more specific terms and agility rules, I recommend you check out some or all of the following organizations:

American Kennel Club: AKC.org
Canine Performance Events: CPE.dog
North American Dog Agility Council: nadac.com
Teacup Dog Agility Association: K9tdaa.com
UK Agility International: UKagilityinternational.com

Agility - A sport where a human and a canine work together as a team to navigate a course within a set amount of time.

Course - Defined by a ring, a course is a series of obstacles set up in a determined manner. They can be set up inside or outside. The flooring must be level and non-slip, and can be made of grass, dirt, rubber, athletic turf, or other similar materials.

Course Maps - These are created by the judges and given to the competitors before the run. Some venues publish the information on the morning of the event, and some may send it out the night before. However, the concept remains the same—competitors do not receive them in advance to train specific skills that may be required. They are more like a pop quiz.

Crosses - Common handling maneuvers, including front, rear, and blind crosses (ways for the handler to move to the opposite side of the dog).

NQ - An abbreviation for when your team does not earn a qualifying score in a run. Some competitors also refer to these as "Not Quites," because it can be the most minor error that causes a team not to qualify.

Obstacles - Refers to things on the agility course that the canine has to perform. Humans guide dogs quickly through obstacles in a predetermined manner. The most common ones are jumps, tunnels, and contacts.

- **Contacts** - Named because they all have a painted yellow "contact zone" that the dog must put a paw in when passing through on their way up and down the obstacle. These include the A-Frame, dogwalk, and teeter.

- **Jumps** - Usually constructed of PVC pipes, jumps are a standard requirement for agility courses. They are set at specific heights, depending on the dog's measured height, typically ranging from four inches to twenty-four inches. There are single, double, and triple jumps, so named for the number of bars that span between the jump frames.

- **Tunnels** - Colorful PVC tubes that come in varying lengths, anchored by sandbags on the course.

Patterning - Practicing something over and over until it becomes second nature. Suitable for certain specific behaviors, but could hinder agility sequences, which are constantly changing.

Q - An abbreviation to signify your team earned a qualifying score in your run. This abbreviation can be both a noun, "We got a Q!" and a verb, "We Q'd in that run!"

Run - An informal term used to describe your turn in the competition. It is a general term that does not specify whether it was a standard course or an agility game. "How did your run go?" "How many runs did you sign up for today?"

Run Order - The trial secretary prints a list of all entered dogs and handlers, grouped by level of competition and run height. Order can switch from small to tall, or tall to small, depending on the venue.

Venue - This word describes which organization or sport you compete in, not necessarily a specific place, as the everyday use of this word would imply. Organizations in the United States that host dog agility trials include AKC, CPE, NADAC, TDAA, and UKI. For specific information, visit their websites, review their mission and vision statements, and browse through their rule books.

About the Author

Virginia Weida is an acclaimed interior designer and CEO & founder of Virginia Weida Designs, established in 2006. She is a certified interior designer, certified facility manager (RCFM), and LEED accredited professional with over thirty years of experience. As a workplace design and project management expert, Virginia collaborates with building owners, brokers, and property managers to deliver creative, budget-conscious solutions that enhance property value. Her unique blend of expertise ensures spaces support occupant health, safety, and success.

A respected CRE industry leader, Virginia is dedicated to service and social impact. She has maintained her lifelong commitment to making a social impact by volunteering with national, regional, and local organizations; supporting her industry, local communities, and small businesses; and uplifting women. She has held president or chair roles in national and local organizations four times in the past five years, served on numerous boards, and taught as adjunct interior design faculty for twelve years. She continues to mentor emerging professionals and advocate for women in business.

Her honors include ASID Fellow (2025), ASID 50 Awardee, 2024 ASID Advocate of the Year, and 2024 ALM|GlobeSt. Woman of Influence (Independent Professional). She is also a published author in the Amazon bestselling anthology *Steps to*

Success: One Aha Moment at a Time and a frequent speaker on design and personal empowerment.

Virginia received her BS in design and environmental analysis from Cornell University. She resides in Pittsburgh, Pa., with her husband and their dachshunds. She is passionate about spending time with her family and her two grown daughters. Virginia is also an avid canine sports competitor and enjoys traveling, wine tasting, reading, music, and the arts.